AF544812

WHAT IS THE MEANING OF MONEY?

Edited by

ROGER-PAUL DROIT

SOCIAL SCIENCE MONOGRAPHS, BOULDER
DISTRIBUTED BY COLUMBIA UNIVERSITY PRESS, NEW YORK
1998

This volume was published with the financial assistance of the French Ministry of Culture

ISBN 0-88033-976-4
Library of Congress Catalog Card Number 98-61691

Printed in the United States of America

TABLE OF CONTENTS

PREFACE

TIME IS MONEY...

From one world to another

Money used to keep in the background and its role remained unacknowledged, though of course inevitable—in an industrialized, urbanised and productive world it played a necessary part—but it was rarely mentioned. Maybe the reason was that it circulated all the time in the shape of coins, notes and signed cheques, which passed from one hand to the next, in a wordless flow.

Yet some important characteristics present in our era were lacking in the earlier one, which nonetheless could be described as modern. People used to listen to the news on transistor radios and not on FM radio. The news broadcasts did not mention the Nikkei index, nor changes in the Dow Jones or fluctuations on the CAC 40. The stock market concerned professionals only. The man in the street did not wake up to learn the point at which Tokyo had closed during the night, nor did he fall asleep knowing how New York had done, or breakfasted live with the Palais Brongniart.

Nor did television, in black and white, then called ORTF (French Radio and Television Organisation) scrutinize every day the Mark, Dollar and Yen exchange rates. The balance of payments and trade deficit were not daily in the news. Tapie, a French Trump was not yet a rich man. There were no programs called "Wheel of Fortune" and "The Price is Right." If a presidential candidate mentioned inflation he had to add quickly "rise in prices" in the knowledge that the former term, far too technical, would not be understood by the electorate at large.

Clearly France twenty years ago was a different world. The BNP (Banque Nationale de Paris) took a bold step in launching an advertising campaign that had a young executive saying: "I'm interested in your money." On the streets many bakeries and cafes had already closed and been replaced by banks. Even so you had to go in to your local branch, speak to an employee and sign a cheque. Machines have changed all this. A card plus a code now ensure that notes come from the hole in the wall. A piece of plastic settles virtually everything, including electronic shopping.

Not so very long ago, a whole range of vocabulary that has now since disappeared was in constant use. There were a number of verbs: "organize," "control," "plan," "supervise," "manage" or even "take precautions," "take charge of" or "face up to," which have been replaced by the ubiquitous "manage." We no longer manage just a portfolio of investments, a business or stocks. We manage our careers, our timetable, our diet, our physical exercise and even our emotions. "I'll be back soon. Can you manage the kids?"—such words are now acceptable. It would not have been so a while back. It is this sort of vocabulary that reveals profound changes in civilization.

There are of course other signs, less anecdotal and more fundamental, of a turning-point occurring in history. Everyone is aware of them and they concern the whole planet: a global market, the computerization of the exchange rate and the stock market, the massive increase of floating capital, the continual launch of new financial products and increase of every type of speculation. At the same time society's attitude to money has changed. For long it remained a taboo subject but has become a symbol, passing from shame to glory, from a contemptible necessity to a fascinating device. Money not only has ceased to be dubious but it is becoming the only value that is understood, and is regarded as the justification of all human activity, or almost. The end of most communist regimes, and above all of the threat of a revolutionary upheaval, has only increased the tendency to view money as the indisputable king, at least for the foreseeable future. One suspects that maybe the king is mad, at the very least suffering from excessive fever and mood changes. Even so this does not stop its holding sway.

These various observations are not novel in themselves. However they cast some light on modern living and it could be useful to examine the question further. It therefore seemed to us entirely appropriate to devote the third "Le Monde Le Mans Forum" to the subject of money in its various forms. Through bringing together researchers and the general public, it is intended to examine in an interdisciplinary and easily accessible way the major topics of our time. Bearing this in mind it seems right to ask what money represents today, to try to see how the various links between financial and illusory reality are organised.

We feel that money is in fact linked to more complex and above all more diverse phenomena than economists suspect. The financial theoreticians and experts, whatever their schools or tendencies, work in abstraction, remaining in reality at a distance from the shady network of feelings, of hopes and despair attached to the power that, in the minds of every on of us, is part and parcel of "Money." No doubt we need to undermine many vague ideas and popular dreams in order to build abstract models and scientific analyses. Yet these elements of dream will never really be dissociated from the monetary mechanism. Everything, be it illusions, rumours, the unpredictable and the anarchic, influences business and contaminates the computer rigour of the financial markets more absolutely than programme viruses. We should take into consideration every facet of the complex notion of money.

This was the first aim we had in mind when initially planing this Forum. Even though this book obviously fails to fulfill such requirements it reinforces its relevance. While preparing it and as the proceedings unfolded, we were confirmed in a conviction that there lies a huge area of research with many questions left to explore. We were surprised that so few studies had up to now focused on this. A few words have to be added in this context to show why this book fits in to the debate.

Exposing a lacuna

Everyone literate person knows that there are books on every subject. Whatever the question, expert publications exist in which specialists argue among themselves. Considering the overreaching importance of money in every human endeavour, above all in today's society, one would expect an inexhaustible bibliography. One would expect to be engulfed in inexhaustible lists of works of every sort, dealing with the history of money, its philosophical and psychological aspects, technicalities and their development, its multiple relationship to the economy, political power, ethics and even art. Yet this overwhelming body of literature does not exist!

There are of course many studies. Some are of a high standard and we are indebted to their authors. But the most striking fact remains that there is an amazing imbalance between the role that money has from a social, historical, and political point of view, and the scarcity of research. It is strange indeed that such an all-pervading element should have aroused so little endeavor from great thinkers in the past. I would venture to assert without even having to check, that over the last 25 years more works have been published about Hamlet or Madame Bovary than on the question of money. Such an enigma needs to be cleared up, if at all possible.

Why are intellectuals, on the whole, thus seemingly blind to the realities of their age? Might it not be that scanning financial news goes against the nobility of theoretical thought. Are these people subject to the old prejudice against ignoble, filthy, despicable or even satanical lucre? It is not impossible even though such an explanation would be simplistic. It might be (and this is no more than a hypothesis) that within the abstract processes that established the symbols of money and language, the status of ideas, the ability to think and spread ideas, there exists a strict contiguity. Money is not an obvious subject in the sense that too many similarities can be observed. It would be a path to follow yet this is not the place to do it.

This book, in fact does not attempt to look for reasons why theoreticians have so consistently shunned the analysis of this fact of life. Its objective is to contribute to a mapping out of the ground or may be give an approximation of the problem. To find out what means, angle and tools we need to start exploring this multiple and fleeting reality which cuts across so many areas. Formulating the basic questions, tracing access routes, defining a phenomenon that is hard to pin down and in to this end drawing on different kinds of expertise; this is the reason for this book coming into being.

It is therefore quite right to take the title of the book quite literally: "How to think of money?" We do not know how, but do try however clumsily to find a way. One would hope to discover a few correct paths. It is not up to us to be the judge of this.

However, it is necessary to emphasize that this Forum is an experiment just as the two previous ones. There are few examples, or perhaps none at all, of gatherings organised by a national daily newspaper, a regional university and the local government. The "Le Monde-Le Mans Forum" is an experiment above all in breaking down barriers between various disciplines, relying on the power of intelligence and clarity, and allowing a wider audience to join in discussion with important researchers from France and abroad.

Nevertheless, over the initial two years this gamble took place within well-defined limits. Whether it was about the new relationship between philosophy and science or on the contemporary study of Greek and Latin, there existed sufficient inquiry, publications and influential writers to enable the experiment to focus on the form rather than the content. The two initial Forums could sketch out a brief inventory of fixtures containing well defined and partially explored problems. It was necessary to highlight and challenge analyses already in existence. On this occasion the experiment must focus on content. It is not a question of filling a lacuna with a study that fits exactly into a black hole of knowledge but rather to reveal a lacuna and realize that in the realm of ideas, Money is still virgin territory.

A book still to be written

The task of committing to a single volume the avenues thus uncovered, the dialogues that took place over the days is highly unusual. The material is varied: some authors revise their texts prior to its delivery, others after, and others still re-read and correct the transcripts of their recorded talks. The free style of the Forum demands that this incongruity in presentation be respected

It is also essential to retain the evidence of discussions that took place. Reproducing them in their entirety was impossible and so only those questions or statements that beg clarification, further consideration or cast a new light are retained. Often summarized they remain faithful to the spirit in which they were offered even though the actual form might have changed.

The short introduction that precedes each chapter, although kept to a minimum, are preferable to a longer text that would have to outline the whole contents of this book. If one keeps these panoramic prefaces in mind whilst reading, one is struck by a slightly unnerving impression of "old hat." Yet if one forgets them come Chapter 2, then what use can they be?

The sittings of the Forum were each focused on a theme followed by general discussion. This format has been respected. The order of the chapters therefore have a coherence and this is offered to the reader. Yet there are other possible avenues. It is up to the reader to invent them. Nothing prevents the reader starting at the end, going on with the middle part, and ending at the beginning. A book waiting to be written, is the task and the privilege of the reader. No doubt this is true of every book but more so of this book since many different trajectories are interwoven. As a consequence, each person can invent their own labyrinth or treasure hunt.

THE NOVEL AND MONEY

Maurice Menard

How can literature, and more particularly the novel, help us to think about the question of money? A passage from the letter dated March 26, 1891, addressed by Huysman to Zola bears witness to the importance of the question while at the same time it reveals the difficulty of an answer. The letter was written a fortnight after the publication in serial form of "Money" in *Gil Blas*:

> It is bustling with people and the battle-ground of the final collapse blazes and sounds like the battle of Sedan. You have really surpassed yourself in portraying those who work at the Stock Exchange as interesting, which they are not. Of course you have made them larger than life and turned Saccard (alias Aristide Rougon) into a terrible and hideous poet.
>
> As for the theory of the book itself that money is a necessary fertilizer for doing great things, it is of course, of all the theories in existence, the simplest and one that can most easily be backed up with arguments. Furthermore you present it in depth and with great panache.
>
> Yet dash it! The more I think about the causes and consequences of money the less, despite the number of more or less reasonable explanations, I understand! What a dashed enigma!
>
> Your book that raises these awesome questions must be mulled over, and that is no mean thing in itself!

The novel form does not give us a theory of money but, using Gilles Deleuze's expression concerning Proust, more important than a theory, it gives us something to ponder. The nineteenth century, the age of the novel and of the conquering bourgeoisie, in fiction attributes to money a dominant role, at least with Balzac and Zola. Balzac and Zola's money, more than any other, is impressive, yet money manifested itself in the novel from the eighteenth century on and the presence of money can be detected in literature down to the twentieth century. Therefore it is the literary expression of money as a whole that we shall examine in answer to the questions it raises for the conduct of our lives.

From the sixteenth century, and especially in dramas, money is portrayed in the form of misers, usurers and then in the seventeenth century bankers: everyone recalls Volpone by Ben Johnson,

Shakespeare's Shylock and Moliere's Harpagon although there are also the portraits of La Bruyere. Nearer to us, money is embodied in Turcaret by Lesage who wrote in 1709. Yet money accurately described makes its true appearance in literature through the novel *Manon Lescaut (1731)* by Abbe Prevost. Manon's "protector" has given her two hundred "pistoles" yet it is she herself that prices her favours: "He kissed my hands more than a million times; it was right that he paid for this pleasure and five or six thousand francs will not be too high a price considering his wealth and his age." Here already money and passion are joined together: passion, ruin and death are intimately bound together. Yet we must wait until Balzac for money to become truly omnipresent in the novel. It precisely because of this that Katherine Mansfield wrote in one of her letters: "When I read Balzac I always feel a particular unpleasant exasperation since according to him everything in life is based on money."

For the first time in literary history, one could read a novel which attempts to strip apart the mechanisms of speculation: *La Maison Nucingen* that initially had as a title *La Haute Banque*. In this short novel, or novelette, written in 1837, the central character is the banker Nucingen, a character who reappears most often in all of the *La Comedie Humaine*. Who could deny its modernity as the character marches through life like a computer making money out of bankruptcy, his own included? In this case gold is not lovingly fondled as with Gobseck or Grandet but is a strategic element, a policy which borders on the political. Balzac wrote that Nucingen had understood something that only today we can understand: that money is power only when it is present in disproportionate quantities. In another novel written in the space of one morning, on January 3, 1844, *Un Homme d'affaires* the game is again exposed. This text, significantly dedicated to "Monsieur Baron James Rothschild, the Consul General of Austria at Paris and banker" relates the exploits of two "carotteurs" which was a slang expression used in the Stock Market meaning a small-time usurer specialising in the purchase at a low price of letters of credit issued by other usurers. Thus Cerizet and Claparon "those two rascals got in touch with Barbet, Chaboisseau, Samanon and other usurers and bought from them hopelessly unsound credit notes." This novel which initially was to be called *Les Roueries d'un creancier* (*The Guile of a Creditor*) highlighted the snowball effects of credit being passed from hand to hand.

Nor was Zola less technical or systematic regarding the use of money as subject matter for novel writing in three of his books—in 1871 *La Fortune des Rougon* and *La Curee* which are the first two novels of the series *Rougon-Macquart* and in 1891 *L'Argent* which is the next but last novel of it. At the beginning, at the centre and at the end money is everywhere and the mechanisms that dictate the Romanesque destiny follow the same curves and the same rhythm as business and the bank. The three Rougon brothers experienced very different endings each according to his ability to seize the chances of history this is the mother of fortune, of power and destiny.

Felicien Marceau was wrong when he concluded that in *La Comedie Humaine* there were no more than five characters for whom money provided the essential drama of life: Grandet, Birotteau, Nucingen, Gobseck and Cerizet. As Balzac wrote in a sentence that Felicien Marceau himself quoted "when living in Paris always keep an eye on the accounts." Money can be seen everywhere in the *Scenes de la vie parisienne* and also in the *Scenes de la vie de province*. Not only in the characters or the novels that specialise in money. It is the same with Zola: money is a factor at the start and at the end of *Rougon-Macquart*, again in *Le Ventre de Paris* or *Au bonheur des dames*, deep in the Voreux *(Germinal)* or else in *L'Assommoir*.

The essential virtue of money in terms of the novel is that it is hidden but present behind the scenes of the story. We easily forget it, though it is the only key to fit the events that are described. Yet all we need to do is re-read the novels for it to appear in its essential reality. We can generally find interwoven into the short summaries of the past that at the start of a Balzac novel lay out as if in passing the dubious speculation at the base of shady or brilliant, happy or tragic lives.

Two examples will suffice to highlight this striking though hidden presence(or perhaps because of this) of the original fortune. In *Pere Goriot*, the "Christ of fatherhood" we have a former pasta maker, a speculator (enterprising enough to buy the business of his employer that fate had made the victim of the first uprising of 1789) an opportunist (whose fortune remained unknown until it was safe to appear rich). The example of *Une double famille* confirms this strange but crucial presence of money at the heart of stories where one would least expect it. One needs to link the humiliating adventures of Judge Granville, abandoned by Caroline Crochard alias de

Bellefeuille, with his "fault" of having entered into a rich marriage without love: he had married the rich, bearded and ugly Miss Bontems. Re-read the letter in which the father advises his son to make this profitable marriage: Bontems senior had been an extreme revolutionary (red bonnet) who of course owned a lot of confiscated property that he bought for a derisory price. But initially he had only had some fields belonging to monks who were never to return; then if you lowered yourself by becoming a barrister then why back away from a further concession to modern ideas. It is the reader's task to remember the origins of this money that was lost in past history. It is impossible to find meaningful the novels that make up *Les Rougon-Macquart* without having read the first of them, *La Fortune des Rougon.* The novel prompts us to assume that money is a censored, fundamentally hidden object, but though always stuffed out of sight it is always present.

An additional reason for taking money into account in novels is that it goes together with dynamism, momentum and creative energy. The force and energy of Balzac and Zola's novels owe a great deal to the theme of money which inspires an epic streak. Both novel and money, awesome machines interpenetrate with diabolical fluidity, each being dragged by the other, in the irrepressible current of the age, permeating the whole of the social scene, covering the whole pyramid, the whole breadth of the spectrum, across the chessboard which Balzac used to lay out his characters. Is there a coincidence between time and money? It appears the "Like time itself, banks devour their children." Is there a coincidence between money and the social structure? Again one can read that at the top stand the houses of Nucingen, Keller, du Tillet and Mongenods; slightly lower down are the Samanons, the Chaboisseaus and the Barbets; then finally, below Mont-de-Piete, a Cerizet the king of usurers hangs about on street corners ready to pounce on miserable people and strangling them all. Balzac's dialectics of the individual and type admirably suits the emphasis put on how money works and vice versa. In all its forms, picturesque or characteristic, money is always there. Furthermore mobility is linked to ubiquity. From being the nerve of war, money becomes the nerve of the written word. Writing about the "carotteur" the words becomes more lively and inflated:

> As their reserve cash they used this fund of slang that is only acquired through a thorough knowledge of Paris, the daring that

> comes from the experience of poverty, the cunning derived from knowing the origin of businesses, of Parisian fortunes, their relations, connexions and the intrinsic value of each person.

As well as this sort of lyrical epic sentences there should also be mentioned the semi-religious litany applied to "the sainted, venerated, strong, amiable, gracious, beautiful, noble, young and all-powerful 100 sous coin."

Yet this cult is often a parody. The novel which thrives on money, and so often takes its impetus, its vitality and sublime energy from money, in the same breath lays the foundation for its downfall and through its verbal excesses manages to deflate its importance. The breathless opening pages of *La fille aux yeux d'or* give an example of this dual effect, of these two sides. The rapid tempo is sustained without flagging throughout the 20 pages dealing with the "energetic pace of Paris" be it the "exaggerated pace of the proletariat" or the "upward movement of money" not to mention the "cyclone of gold." Yet the "physiognomy" of Paris which is described as a "queen," "the leader of the world" and at the same time "a brain that is dying from excess genius." Decay and death are already visible:

> This hollow existence, this everlasting waiting for pleasures that never materialize, this permanent boredom, this silliness of mind, body and heart, the weariness of Parisian entertaining is engraved on their features, giving the cardboard faces premature wrinkles, making the physiognomy of the rich distorted with impotence, only to reveal the image of gold and the absence of all intelligence.

Zola expressed himself in the same epic vein in his description of empty glory. In *La Curee* we can hear like an echo of "gold and pleasure" experienced by *La Fille aux yeux d'or* which turns into "the ring of gold and flesh." Who could better have portrayed better and in this style the divine and human character present in a drama concerning "incest developing on the compost of millions of men and women." Zola, like Balzac before him, knew how to write about the modern golden calf, in this case the Agricultural Credit and Savings Account, in a style that is both lyrical and critical:

> [in this] solemn and dignified temple to money nothing strikes the public with such religious force as the Savings Account where a corridor of sacred austerity led to and one could glimpse

> the safe, the crouching deity, built into the wall, squat and tranquil, with its three locks, its thick sides and its aura of divine beast.

What is perhaps surprising, but which no doubt can be explained, are the contrasting fate the works of Balzac and Zola met with in later years. Both works have been partly affected by the opinions their authors were supposed to hold: there emerges two opposing ideologies represented by Balzac's money and Zola's money. It is assumed that Balzac's ideal portrayed in so many characters was riches and power. Zola the champion of the people could only be opposed to money! Yet the "good" heroes of the *Comedie Humaine* are not the moneyed people: they are either Judge Popinot, the guardian angel of the Saint Marcel district, or the lawyers Chesnel and Mathias who are so upright, or doctor Bianchon, or Joseph Bridau, the model of the unselfish artist or Arthez who experiences glory in poverty. It is the same with the more spiritual characters: Veronique Graslins who is solely intent on her redemption, Felicite des Touches who enters into the order of Saint Francois de Sales and spends her fortune on recovering the land of Calyste Du Guenic. The two main characters of *L'Envers de l'histoire contemporaine,* Madame de La Chanterie and Mr. Alain devote themselves entirely to good works. A similar unselfishness is found in Zola with Doctor Pascal, the only one of the three Rougon brothers who remains totally unaffected by money. A further degree is reached in *L'Argent* with Sigismond, Busch's brother, who casts money to eternal fire: "this horrible money, making the poor suffer." Yet the point of view that this novel repeatedly expresses is far from downright condemnation and this is precisely what Huysman observed in his letter quoted at the start of this text. In fact the words are first those of Saccard and are then echoed by Miss Caroline with some emphasis:

> she recalled her former theories; the necessity of a gamble in large businesses, where fair wages are unrealistic and speculation is seen as the price to pay, a necessary compost, the fertilizer from which progress can flower.

Further on:

> He was right: money had been up until now the compost in which future humanity could grow; money, poisoner and destroyer, was becoming the catalyst of all social growth, the

> necessary compost for large projects that facilitate existence. Why attribute to money the blame for the dirt and crime which it causes.

The person who reads Balzac too fast or one unaccustomed to his style would never notice or recall the other side of the medal, its destructive power. With Zola the only part that is remembered is the accusation he leveled at money. The careful arch-reader of either will see that both considered money as the subject most likely to arouse a feeling of ambivalence, of pro and con. It is the ideal framework for tension in a novel and brings about in the reader a reaction of both desire and revulsion.

Psychoanalysts would say that this duality is characteristic of all our drives. This third field of enquiry promises rich pickings and shows money to be endowed with universal attraction, it is a monster that conjures up fantasies on a par with sex, both in the main being linked to each other.

This aspect of the question was to strike Maupassant sharply when he read *Manon Lescaut*. In a preface to the novel he quotes this significant passage which shows that there is no frontiers between money and the pleasures of love:

> Never was there a woman so little in love with money yet she could not ever be at ease for fear of being short. What she wanted was pleasure and something to pass the time of day. She never wanted to touch a sou it had been possible to enjoy oneself without spending anything. She did not try to find out what was the basis of our wealth [...] yet it was something so essential for her, to be thus leading a life of pleasure that it was impossible to make the least demand on her humour or inclination without it.

Maupassant goes on to say that for Manon "money and love were one and the same thing."

Money, for Manon, was present but hidden behind love, in a way it was a part of it but dormant and implicit. With Balzac money is more forthcoming. Nucingen the banker, the fat bumblebee in love, bases his hope to possess Esther on his wealth and declares it with self congratulation in his thick Germanic accent: "How right I am to have lots of money!" Crevel measures his love for Valerie Marneffe by the gold standard: "I do not love you, Valerie," says Crevel. "I love you like a million gold sovereigns."

Like love, money that is dreamed about is a mad currency which is almost miraculous. A fortune is never able to satisfy our dreams as one that comes unexpectedly, a gift from the gods. Danae's golden downpour or the flow of the jackpot it is the gift of the gods. It has been said that money is immoral if won while one is asleep. Yet this is the condition for it to fulfill our dreams and seem truly fairy-like. The novel also acquaints us with this fact. Zola gives Aristide Rougon (the future financier called Saccard) this quasi magical dream of a fortune: "He saw himself a millionaire ten times over; he earned barrels of gold from one day to the next." Balzac gratifies Rastignac with considerable wealth, more precious still as it was unexpected and incomprehensible: "He could not understand how but he had won 400,000 francs." Nucingen the wizard had orchestrated everything.

This fantasy grips up with all the might of the drive for survival, drawing its strength from the death wish which it is associated with. The story of *La Peau de chagrin* teaches this lesson and Zola's novels confirm it. For Saccard, in *L'Argent* "to climax is perhaps no more than be feeding on one's own flesh" and again, when Pierre Rougon suddenly has a destructive and flaming red and gold vision: "He thought he saw a glimpse, like a bolt of lightening, of the future of the Rougon-Macquarts, a pack of desires loosed and sated, in a flame of gold and blood."

Novels thus help us to realize the power of money in those very moments when, bordering on myth, it displays its multiple facets: in the sequence of time, in the dynamics of action and language, and in the phantasmagory of imagination.

It would be easy to quote the many examples that are present in novels, of outspoken and outright condemnation of money, in particular of money dishonestly obtained. In the face of the excesses of Manon and des Grieux, Tiberge says indignantly:

> Is it possible, he says to me, that the wealth that you use to sustain your licentiousness could have been attained by legitimate means? You have acquired it unfairly and it will be taken away from you in the same way. God's most horrible punishment would be to allow you to enjoy it undisturbed.

Yet can this condemnation of "filthy lucre" help us have a clearer idea of the question of money? No doubt no more than the words of Victor Hugo in praise of "honest money" which is expressed in the words of Jean Valjean: "What hurt me, Mister

Pontmercy, was that you did not want to use this money.... It is honestly earned. You can be rich with an easy mind."

In every passage of condemnation or unadulterated praise, the novel wilts, at least the kind that Cervantes inaugurated and which Kundera rightly developed.

In every instance when money is put under scrutiny, in order that the condemnation might provide food for thought and encourage us to push further along this uncomfortable avenue, criticism must be indirect and in the form of a negation. First among these anti-heroes of money stand the truculent parasites that have regularly appeared in western literature since the sixteenth century. Falstaff in the *Merry Wives of Windsor* and elsewhere, Rameau's nephew and Fourchon from *Les Paysans*: poor heroes who are not even true to type and honest with themselves, provocative heroes, who criticize wealth although they covet it greatly. Money needs to be present so that, this idea of contented poor can be engendered, in opposition to and independent from money, a challenge to yet at the same time the guarantors of the established order. These contradictory figures allow a perspective on money as a valuable yet derisory source of pleasure. This symbolism echoing Menippeas avoids the pitfalls of straight moralizing.

Stendhal and Flauberts' fables could have also interesting facets to contribute. Neither *Le Rouge et le Noir* nor *La Chartreuse de Parme* concern money. Julien Sorel died, Madame de Renal was to die three days later but Mathilde de La Mole survived and the cave where she buried Julien's head with her own hands was on her instructions "adorned with very expensive Italian marble statues." By the end of *La Chartreuse* Sandrino, Clelia, Fabrice and La Sanseverina were dead. All the heroes dear to Beyle and his readers died. Mosca survived "immensely wealthy." The ending of each novel reveals its real significance through the discreet use of the symbolism of money, essential though barely expressed. It figures as an trivial detail, but casts its blinding light in retrospect on the whole construction. As for *Madame Bovary* one must realize that this novel dealing with unrequited love is also about debt, about money matters and although there is no overt adverse judgment the facts of the plot condemn the power of money. Finally where would Frederic Moreau, Bouvard and Pecuchet stand without the added interest of inheritance?

In the twentieth century the best novels concerning wealth are those where it is hidden. In the Ferral-Valerie episode of the *Condition Humaine*, behind the eroticism of humiliation and bondage there runs the golden thread of money. On a similar theme Georges Perec's *Les Choses* can be seen as the best example of the era of consumerism and money ruling over men. In the "popular" novel of the type *Billet vert* or in adverts that try to create a demand, never before has money been treated as subject and show. Whether cast in the role of the devil or benefactor money is the center of attention. We are surrounded with images that are overflowing with gold: women dressed in gold, golden overflowing chocolates, fish fingers which represent the captain's gold, cars with a golden guarantee or the jewelry departments of department stores.... Yet the "golden boys" and the "yuppies" are no longer fashionable and we tone down the sound during the adverts on the television. There are signs that we are returning to the critical role of the novel, providing a mirror that examines life in detail, making us plunge and distance ourselves. Thus we can be surrounded by money thanks to the novel but also thanks to it be cured.

The Symbolic Franc

Alain de Mijolla

Among all the ways one might consider dealing with the subject of money I have tried to limit myself to the psychological aspects adopting a Freudian approach. In other words to question whether psychoanalytical theories help us to "Think about money at present" in a slightly different way, and how? A further limitation should be added to that of time: "within western culture," since I have little knowledge of others such as eastern or far eastern ways of thinking.

"Money does not bring happiness" is a popular expression and we all know the "but it helps." Freud without signaling it out specifically, one day commented on this saying in a letter to his friend Wilhelm Fliess: "Happiness is the realisation of a deep-rooted childish wish. This is the reason why wealth contributes so little to it. Money is not an object of a child's desire" (Freud S., 1950, 16 January 1889). It is no doubt also the reason why there are so few psychoanalytical studies about it, which I discovered in preparing this paper and which leads me today to speak to you not so much as the spokesman of "Psychoanalysis," with a capital P, but in my own name. Not only because there are so many schools of thought that claim to be psychoanalytical and I cannot hope to be acquainted with all their theories, or do them justice, or give a faithful account, but also because a psychoanalyst can only approach such a subject from a subjective point of view, whether he likes it or not.

Even so, a little history prior to considering "today." Be this only because of the two temporal references which we have to have when we want to interpret a phenomenon and attempt to reconstruct the unconscious significance: the past and the present, these two "pillars of dream" that Freud described to his patient Dora.

Concerning an individual's past as well as that of psychoanalysis, it should be remembered that in 1908, having drawn conclusions on the eroticism of the anal region put forward in *Three Essays on Sexual Theory,* Freud established a link, which the unambiguous poster of this conference shows as universally accepted: "In reality, wherever archaic thought held sway or remains, in ancient civilisations, in myths, fairy tales, superstitions and in unconscious thought, money is intimately linked to excrement" (Freud S., 1908a).

During 1914-18, Freud completed his description by connecting this initial interpretation with that of the "present." Defecating appears as an intense moment that joins the child to its primordial objects, with its two contradictory sides: love, in obeying parental instructions about anal education, hatred in contrast, refusal and individual enjoyment by its retention which worries and exasperates those around. He wrote:

> It is reasonable to assume that it is not "gold-money" but "present-gift" which is the initial reason for interest in excrement. The child does not know any other currency apart from what is given to him. He is unaware of the capacity of earning money, of the existence of one's own money or inherited money. Excrement being its first present, the child easily transfers its interest in this substance to this new substance which in its life seems to be the most important present. (Freud S., 1917c.)

We need only skim over the associations that lead to an equivalence: present-child-penis, all joined together to form the "unconscious concept" of "small." Or in other words what can be separated from the body (Freud S., 1918b), to emphasize, along with the other psychoanalysts that were Freud's contemporaries, an interpretation in anal terms of fantasies that specifically involve money. According to Sandor Ferenczi, one of the most original among them:

> Following on from the feeling of pleasure that the contents of the intestine give, we end up concluding that money gives us joy. Yet according to this money is in fact no more than deodorized excrement. Dried out and polished; pecunia non olet: money has no smell. In parallel to the rational progress of the intellect, the symbolic interest of the adult for money is no longer limited to objects that have the physical characteristics of coins but extends to all sorts of things that signify in one way or another possession (paper money, shares, savings accounts etc.). Money can have many forms, however the joy of possessing it is rooted most profoundly and fruitfully in coprophilia. Sociologists and political economists when examining the facts objectively need to bear in mind this irrational element. Social problems can only be resolved through identifying the real human psyche. Speculation about economic conditions will never lead anywhere on its own. (Ferenczi S., 1914.)

These lines were written in 1914 and no doubt we would be less assertive nowadays, even though there has been a slow infiltration of psychoanalytical notions into every aspect of culture, be it only to refute it, and even unwittingly influences sociology and economics. In the way that was intentional from the very beginning a vocabulary of psychoanalysis was invented with a crucial place given to meta-psychological considerations such as the "economic point of view," notions of quantity that dominate the dynamics of psychic processes, or "investment" which is a term both military and financial in German as well as in French.

Since these early symbolic interpretations of money and the others such as finding the roots of its attraction in such and such a stage of the libidinal development of the child have flourished. I need only quote as an example "greed" with its oral origins implied by thirst for possession, the urinary associations that the image of liquid money (cash) evokes, the phallic connotations that characterize its showy exhibitionism, aggressiveness with its anal origins that is part of most financial dealings. Not to mention the images that are suggested by dirty money, money laundering etc. I would emphasize in considering equivalences and interpretations the reference to the Freudian myth of the father of the primitive tribe who is the sole owner of wealth and where the maternal body is considered as the prototype of all lost property and remains always unrecovered. It also appears that it is basically when making character type descriptions that the theme of money is most easily approached: the miser for whom money is something to accumulate; the spendthrift who can only enjoy what is his by spending it, etc.

For it would seem that the notion of money raises a multitude of associations each more ingenious and more "true" than the others. This polysemy in any case bears witness to its importance in man's psychic reality and to all the unconscious echoes that it evokes—always later on, since as we have seen money is not the object of a childhood desire

Its impact in fact only becomes significant at the start of the Oedipal complex in what is unhappily termed the latent phase even though it had previously attracted the child's attention as a possible "treasure"; a collectable object. Made more attractive as it seemed to represent a field reserved for adult members of the family and is at the core of frequent and emotional discussions. To be precise, I would maintain that money, as a material, is more or less precociously, and even obsessively, the object of play activity. However, the "notion of money" only manifests itself at a later date. This apparition goes hand in hand with the prominent place given to of feelings of tenderness in emotional relationships that were stormy initially and with implanting in everyone of us the sense of an authority that portrays itself as above the self and as the representative of a law without which life would be impossible.

The link between money and the metamorphosis of the two main drives—the erotic and the urge to destroy—only takes place later which means that it can take on the multiplicity of meanings that have been suggested. The sense of money follows the footsteps of the ability to perceive things in abstract terms -for even more than language acquisition it is this evolution to an abstract language that is contemporaneous—as a method of distancing emotional drives which otherwise are hard to control. Like a third party that mediates in the emotional relationship of dependency which the developing Oedipal complex has pushed to the furthest point and shown the limits and consequences of its fantasies.

The acquisition of a sense of money takes place at the same time as the process of becoming autonomous and desexualized, part of which is known as "sublimation." This "small thing," detachable, exchangeable, collectable seems like a late substitute used for everything, just as alcohol or drugs, yet with this essential difference that it takes its place outside the subject, outside the body itself. We have said that it is a third party which together with its polysemy allows it to play a symbolic but absolutely essential role in some of the important processes of human existence.

Due to the little time available, I will not consider all of them, yet I will describe some to sow the seed for further discussion.

Firstly the notion of inheritance. No human being is born without inheriting from their progenitor something that materially might be outlined in a will yet only forms a representation of an external reality. Other than our genetic VXK" we inherit in fact a tradition, a genealogy and a fantasy past that during the course of our lives we explore like the children of La Fontain's peasant forever ploughing the land and which we ourselves in turn transfer either directly or indirectly. The way in which families consider money is part of the identifiable supports with which little by little the subject manages to form itself and nobody, in this area as in others, can escape his destiny nor the inequalities and fickleness of birthrights. Assets or liabilities, success, savings or fraud, nobody is untouched by the sagas or corpses hidden under the bundles of notes in the unconscious cupboards of our progenitors. I emphasized this point in another context (Mijolla A. de, 1981) and therefore do not need to say any more today.

Another theme that we can only skim over is that of debt. We find ourselves from the start and at the most intimate level in a situation of indebtedness, which Shakespeare underlines: "Thou owest God a death."

Indebted for the gift of life, we owe nature (as Freud by mistake wrote, such was his loathing of the idea of invoking a God in human history...) a death, our own, and one understands better how money can come to characterize one of the symbolic attempts that man makes to redeem, before it is too late, such an onerous debt. Since all monetary transactions, from the simplest -buying some bread to survive—as well as the most sophisticated financial deals, can be seen as equivalent, on a socio-cultural level, by those who believe they can settle it in good time, as a victory over death, be it at the risk of a heart attack. If one has to "pay one's way in life" is it not permissible by the same token to hope for sufficiently disproportionate gains to buy one's own immortality? Mephistopheles has been succeeded by frozen coffin salesmen, yet the market for Faustian candidates is still very much alive....

This "debt of life" with its accompanying conflicts, since as has already been said we also inherit liabilities from preceding generations, is in effect something that we come across very frequently in therapy. It entails love, gratitude or very often grudges and hatred directed at parents who were more or less willing accomplices in usury or their equivalent. Clearly, turned round, this lies at the heart of the well known demand where "I did not ask to be born" is a prelude to repeated demands for something that is owing, which the family environment however generous (in a naive attempt to smooth its bad conscience) will fail to compensate for. On another register the oft-repeated interpretations of a psychoanalysis which has been taken hostage, or even the subsidies of the welfare state which is bound to be seen as inadequate in any case.

Every negotiation has to have an intermediary or a third party. This is where money comes into play over and above its genetic significance which have been designated as "anal," "oral," "phallic" or whatever else one wants it to be. It intervenes as the necessary third party, sufficiently figurative (one only has to think of the royal profiles on coins or the great historical figures on banknotes) to see that it has a family/cultural origin, yet at the same time abstract enough in that it depends on the quantity for it to assume the role of a sort of interchangeable "joker."

The symbolic value of money, as we can see, is in the field where the classic notion of exchange can be replaced by a more egoistic, or narcissistic (as we say in the jargon) procedure.

It seems to me that this occurs through the means of quantity or more especially of the complementary elements formed by the unit and the many. The code of money by its abstraction unites everything and everybody under a common denominator which will appear to some as God, Hell or the cosmos but clearly representing a mirror image of the subject himself in its idealised form. Money for each of us is above all a portrait of ourselves, even if we like to stress the element of parental protection that it also represents so as to answer the need never to be without it in order to exist precisely as individuals. The miser, by locking it away in a safe, protects his own identity from intrusion. It is his personality that the prodigal man throws away and it is to be a "good father figure" that the wise man manages his small nest-egg, his child, the child that he was or would have liked to be.... Tell me how you think about and what you do with money and I will tell you who you are.

No doubt I am speaking from a very narrow point of view. Money has its place in the process of psychoanalytical treatment. Many jokes show this and the witticism of La Bruyere readily comes to mind: "As long as people can die but want to live, the doctor will be scoffed at and well paid."

Money in fact plays a part in talk, dreams and actions of the patient, like those of the psychoanalyst, being the "material" to interpret throughout the treatment, similar to everything else and having a specific place that is important in the up and downs of transfer and counter-transfer (which in itself has a very financial ring to it at least in French). It is never without significance that the patient forgets to pay for the session, makes mistakes in his accounts, expects his analyst to give back the change, stuffs crumpled and dirty notes into his hand or, while appearing to look elsewhere, leaves an envelope containing new notes, that look as if they have been freshly ironed, on the edge of a piece of furniture. Each behaviour in relation to money/substance and the obligation to pay has its origin in the history of the subject as well as in the history of their psychoanalytical journey. It is the business of the psychoanalyst to discover conscious associations and unconscious portrayals.

Yet the "notion of money" in the treatment, once again to establish the distinction, is slightly different. The need to pay was precociously displayed by Freud as early as 1913 in one of the few articles that he wrote dealing with "analytical technique." This work was called "The Start of the Treatment":

> At the early stage of the analytical treatment there are two very important questions that need to be asked: how long and how much. In terms of time I believe that it is absolutely essential to decide on a fixed hour. Each of my patients is given an hour of my working day; this hour belongs to them and is charged for even if they fail to use it. [...] An analyst has no intention to deny that money should, above all else, be seen as a means of living and gaining power, yet he would also claim that important sexual factors play a role in the assessment of money. This is why he expects to see civilized people dealing with the question of money in the same way as with sexual acts; with the same duplicity, shame and hypocrisy. This is why the doctor from the start should refuse to play along with this and deal with the question of money with as much natural frankness as he would expect from his patient over sexual matters. By speaking straight out of his fee and working out how much each hour that he spends with his patient is worth, the practitioner shows him that he renounces false shame. [...] I believe that it is more dignified and morally correct to recognize one's demands, one's real needs, rather than pose as disinterested philanthropists, as doctors still pretend to be, whereas they cannot afford it and suffer silently or complain loudly about the lack of consideration and miserliness of their patients. By showing the amount that he earns, the analyst can claim that his hard work never permits him to earn as much as other specialist doctors. [...] Free treatment results in an increased resistance and for example among young women, one sees that this can lead to temptation in the stage of transfer; with young men one notes a revolt against the obligation of being indebted, a revolt that stems from the parental complex which is one of the most serious obstacles to treatment. The absence of the corrective influence of payment has serious disadvantages; the whole relationship is remote from the real world; deprived of a good reason to end the treatment, the patient no longer feels the same desire for a conclusion. (Freud S., 1913.)

Free psychoanalytical treatment has continued to arouse debate and comment among societies of psychoanalysts which I can not go into. Several solutions have been put forward to reconcile the irreconcilable. On the one hand, fairness would demand that one gives financial help to the poor so that they might benefit from analysis and hence the creation of "treatment centres." Since Freud's era, in Vienna for some time, there was an obligation to treat at least one patient free or else payment by organisation such as social security. On the other hand, it is necessary to remember the unique nature of the psychoanalytical relationship, apparently dual but which works due to the presence of a third party. This third party is not in reality present in the session but is fictionally there and helps both sides to exchange mental representations, continually to shift position and relive forgotten childhood scenes.

If this third party takes the form of an official inspector who interferes with this reality asking for accounts of the treatment taking place, judging the progress or results, ready to stop his support or set conditions, then strictly-speaking psychoanalytical work is no longer possible.

Completely free treatment is almost impossible as Freud clearly pointed out its serious drawbacks. Payment is an indispensable means to distance each in this close relationship that joins the analyst and the analyzed. Money assumes the role of an external reality that during the latent period guarantees a return to self-reliance at the end of every session whatever fantasy bullying might have preceded.

I would say that money is a barrier to excessive suggestion which is a danger in every relationship of transfer. Patients do not try to get "something" material from the psychoanalyst (although they might find it) they try and find their "being." It is also there that money comes in, representing themselves, which they give to the analyst as the price for their new acquisition. It is the clearest means of "paying for themselves" and of course this is very different from the pernicious stories that portray having to pay the analyst to suffer and that the more you pay the better it works and other rubbish like that.

Once again, since it seems to me to be so very important in the psychoanalytical relationship, it should be stressed that money is above all one of our most important representations. It is also more concrete since it is hidden under an apparently universal symbolism and is the object of social exchanges.

This excessive subjectivity might seem surprising even though, since much has been made of the objectivity of the values that it allows for, of the unifying of qualities that is represented by their change into quantity, of the increasing abstraction that this development leads to. Also I return to those questions that reading Georg Simmel's *Philosophy of Money* as well as the various ideas that since 1900, and especially those of Serge Moscovici incorporated into his book, *La Machine a fabriquer des dieux* (*The Machine that Creates Gods*). Yet I feel that we could round off these exciting questions with the following question: are not the infinite multiplication of numbers just as the unending increase in quantity, in fact just part of the whole, or in other words, in psychoanalytical terms, which are difficult to avoid here, part of the narcissistic fantasy of the subject which, like so many others, several years ago I outlined as: "I am everything. I am unique"? (Mijolla A. de, 1984).

Harpagon does not only fear the loss of his casket as a "treasure" that is separate from himself. His cries are heart-rending and stir something within us, despite the fact that it is set within a farce, for we perceive that really his money represents him, like a wax doll might do, and he feels dismembered, dispossessed of himself, of an excessive narcissistic representation far removed from any sort of excremental game. One would have to be completely ignorant of what goes on in casinos nor have seen the faces and attitudes of those who are desperately involved with cards or chips, sometimes without any physical contact, to remain unaware of what is really "at stake." Destiny is challenged, hence the figure of the parent is involved, but money which is supposed to overcome it (or with the help of a bit of masochism to be destroyed in the process) is identified with the subject.

No sum of money, however disproportionate it might be, would for Shylock be worth the pound of flesh that belongs less to Antonio's body than to the idea that he has of himself. Those who read into this pathetic court case only the cruelty of a bitter Jewish usurer are missing what is really at stake. Only something approximating to "Unique," something symbolically equivalent to himself, like a cheque destined to pay his debt of birth—with all that at that time being born Jewish would mean to him—only this much would have been sufficient to satisfy him.

This is what a shrewd legislator (being wholly ignorant of how it came into being I would be very grateful if I were given information about this) managed to do when the notion of a "symbolic franc" was invented as a way to repair the battered self-ego of the subject. That is where it is so clever for it keeps the whole process on the level of the *symbolic*. By maintaining the necessary misunderstanding that protects the presence of the subject himself, in the flesh, throughout the tort, litigation and reparation. In any case it is well known that once one leaves the realm of the symbolic in calculating the amount of disability or *praetium doloris* one enters into a process of never-ending claim and counterclaim.

Every poison has its antidote and in a world which following the collapse of egalitarian or communist utopias some feel is destined to become a hell enslaved by the god Moloch of money, the existence of such symbolic transactions seems to me to give hope. That the franc through the idea of "one" and only "a single one" is used instead of the person itself, and in its image of a circle guarantees an idealized return to wholeness, this seems to me to be a very important advance for civilization, which should be emphasized. In the old days, a debt was paid for by letting blood and causing death (the Corsican vendetta still exists) but the settling of accounts has become the subject of a secular ceremony that rests on contractual equivalents between people of a similar civilization.

Such a development is rather comforting in a world that otherwise might seem overburdened with cruel financial wars. These, however seemingly cruel, might really be less atrocious than that of a lone man, his body suffering and deprived of a shield/representative, turned into a pawn at the mercy of faceless interests that confront each other throughout the world for the fantasy of power.

Thus Freud wrote to Albert Einstein in 1932 in *Warum Krieg* one should not believe that the antagonism of the two impulses of life and death should ever disappear, nor that violence could evaporate, aggression and the wish to wipe out anyone who is a threat to one's possessions, money or life. At most what we could hope for, and this is the work cut out for our generation as well as generations to come, is to codify its manifestations and privilege even more distant substitutes. Money with this in mind seems a particularly well-suited medium for such transactions or contractual precautions. Yet, even so we should not be deceived. The very fact that money represents the person, with their conflicting urges, inner conflicts in which the conscious and unconscious are mingled, makes of this completely abstract object, which is nothing but a game of numbers in which logic should rule, the scene of the most irrational behaviour, be it individually or as a group. But it is also because it comes at a late stage of the libidinal development of man that it constitutes a breakwater forever weak or near to breaking under the battering caused by the tendency to regression.

Yet it is precisely because it has a past deep in human history that one can make it a subject for discussion, this conference proves it. A person who juggles with billions on the computer or faxes sibylline orders that destroy empires on the other side of the world, is not immune to discovering this history within himself: all he has to do is go out of the office just to buy the paper, search his pocket for change and the vendor will thank them in return.... Anything might bring out, as in Orson Welles' *Citizen Kane* a personal *Rosebud*. Each person's past, be they the most implacable financier, is irrepressible and its rising to the surface impossible to control, even though like Howard Hughes one might try to shore up the breaches through which it might once again spring forth.

I count on the human aspect of the portrayal of oneself that is implied in money, therefore on the unconscious irrational processes that are involved, to give life and Eros to what so many Cassandras have promised will be a universe governed by her Majesty Money and devoted to abstract inhuman financial battles. I believe more in this than in the virtues of some new ideology that is supposed to preserve us from the ever-present ambiguities of money, whether hiding behind the mask of religion or based on another theory which ends in "ism."

Yet I am straying from my appointed task and Max Weber obligingly provides me with a conclusion which will restore me to a more modest position, that of a psychoanalyst which I ask you to forgive me for having on occasion forgotten:

> It is true that human destiny is nothing but shocking to anyone who examines only a specific period. But it is correct to keep little personal comments to oneself in the same way as when seeing the sea or a mountain, unless one feels a vocation and a special gift to express them in the form of a work of art or a prophesy. In almost all other cases the wordiness of "intuitive" discourse only hides the fact that one is unable to keep a distance in relation to the object. Such an inability should be judged in the same way whenever this lack of perspective is applied to mankind. (Weber M., 1947.)

Westernization of the World

An Encounter of Monetary Representations: A Dual Illusion

Jean-Michel Servet

We are told that during the Egyptian campaign, Bonaparte's soldiers were asked to pay for their purchases with the buttons from their uniforms. Indeed it was customary for many of the local population to pierce coins and sew them to their clothes. These buttons were taken as the coinage of the European occupiers. Egypt had by the end of the eighteenth century been using coins for well over two thousand years: Ionian sovereigns during the Hellenistic period and later foreign forces and monarchs had minted them down the ages. Both participants, western and eastern, in this strange transaction were familiar with numismatic practices; the faces, persons or animals represented on French coins perhaps offended the Muslim population which was more accustomed to geometrical designs on their coins. Hence the preference for buttons and their place on clothes might also have made them seem like coins. The foreigner is usually understood with reference to oneself. Means of payment are not divorced from this rule. Nevertheless Egypt and western Europe by the end of the eighteenth century, besides having a shared history at a time and relations going far back into the past, did have some similarity in their culture, especially political and economic structures, which were comparable.

So when the British, Germans, Dutch, Spanish, French, Portuguese or Russians colonized the societies that, as a whole, form what we call today the third world, they rarely encountered or conquered societies "without money." This is clear not only in the North African or Middle Eastern civilisations who were distant heirs of ancient monetary traditions, or of India and the Far East where numismatic traditions are perhaps older than those of Greece or Asia Minor, but also societies such as the Mayans, the Aztecs or the Sudanese where cloth and cocoa for the former, and cowry shells for the latter, were recognized means of payment. However varied the traditions of means of payment might have been, with concomitant usage of various ways of settling accounts and a combination of the process of accounting with that of paying, over and above these exotic forms and usages, currencies had a similarity with that of the colonizers in respect to their being instruments to serve societies organized under a central government. Their fiscal role in particular permitted a form of dialogue that was favourable to colonization, and the Europeans cleverly used to their own advantage some of the local institutions and structures. In the main they initially agreed to collect taxes and pay for some expenditures with "native" currencies. Coins and notes gradually replaced these in time. In some cases, the law speeded up this process by forbidding the use of the old money in state transactions, and the bemused locals saw the Europeans publicly destroying assets which only a few months, weeks or even days before they had harshly demanded as taxes. This measure was only taken when the colonial power felt confident enough and wanted to eradicate for ever local political forces hostile to their rule. Although these ancient monies disappeared from official transactions, and from most business transactions, some traditional uses were to remain for a long time notably in matrimonial alliances, compensation for murder and ritual offerings to fetishes.

The situation of course was very different when first travelers or explorers, then conquest and colonial occupation brought Europeans into contact with radically different cultures, communities which were supposedly classless and without a state, that would not have known about currency but used a barter system.

Prior to analyzing the interpretations that were given of our own system of payment in these societies, we propose briefly to describe the local methods of payment; in so doing we will give the "point of view of the vanquished," in other words the mental framework through which the colonized understood the colonizers, while at the same time showing the ethnocentric nature of the Westerner. A common store of knowledge was lacking between the two sides in this encounter. Yet each was unaware of this fact and believed that the other side understood in the same way the act of reciprocity. Both side were under this illusion. Illusion and scorn of the colonials for the "primitive currencies" to which they attributed functions and assets analogous to our own monetary systems. Illusion and scorn on the part of the colonized who felt our coins and notes were really the same as their own "monetary" instruments. This dual illusion was engendered by the identification of a foreign practice or object with known practices and objects. In this case on the one hand an instrument of the market place and on the other a means of social exchange, and to apportion to them a specific role arising from the category to which this object or practice was presumed to belong.

With increasing contact and intimacy the differences were gradually understood; a shared knowledge meant that relations could be reorganised. Even so, even now despite the forced modernisation and voluntary imitation, financial practices (such as informal savings and credit practices—*tontines*) remain and even spread which would seem irrational in the eyes of western businesses and reflect inherited social and mental norms that have been transformed to answer the imperatives of the times.

"PRIMITIVE" MONETARY PRACTICES

It is necessary to explain here two antithetical *a priori* phenomena that were described by travellers: the practice of barter and the existence of "primitive coinage." It is usual to read in books written in the nineteenth century that colonized people or those about to be colonized only had very limited scope for trade and, either cause or consequence, there did not arise a need to use currency. These populations were the living remnants of a pre-monetary age which is seen as corresponding to an initial barter system.

In fact, the exchange practices of these populations that were seen as "primitive" were infinitely more complicated that the westerners could imagine. Since time immemorial products crossed the continents. Products from the south of Australia reached the northern coast of New Guinea. The so called primitive societies did not exchange a hypothetical over-production but produced goods with exchange in mind. These products became the favoured means of payment for goods produced by other groups (be it bark capes, blocks of salt, stone axes etc.). Furthermore in these supposedly classless cultures some communities—this phenomenon was seen in Amazonia as well as in the western Pacific—specialized in the role of commercial intermediary. Finally one should emphasize that these "primitive" commercial practices must be regarded as social interaction, in other words as relations between groups and individuals who either wage war on each other or not, maintain matrimonial relations or not, share myths and religions or not, who eat together or not etc., from which arises a protocol of exchanges, rites, words, agreed signs that are the product of a distant past; in particular the price of the exchanged goods is generally a secondary variant in the transaction in terms of the whole system of reciprocal obligations.

Westerners tended to be ignorant about this diplomatic aspect of exchanges the reasons for which they ignored. Hence sometimes they would refuse to trade and acts were committed, possibly reciprocal, that were considered by one or other of the parties as theft, violence etc. The setting up of permanent trading posts, the imposition of relations, the introduction of new products (for example the metal ax) completely disrupted the ancient trading networks and in most cases destroyed them, in the same way as the traditional means of payment that were accepted in bilateral relations. Thus there developed between the colonized and the colonizers first an economy based on exchange and then the slave trade.

In parallel to pre-colonial trade relations who's importance western travellers underestimated and failed to understand the reasons for, was in circulation some very strange precious goods: shell collars or bracelets, pearls, teeth, stones, indigenous metals, feather rolls, polished stone disks etc. products of local craftsmen or else imported. Why were these objects seen as "primitive currency" by westerners? These objects that appeared quite uniform did not at first sight have any use per se (for food, dress, work or war) other than to pass between groups or individuals and thus appeared to base their utilitarian value on their exchange value. Hence why they are called currencies. It is obvious that since money was considered as an attribute of superior forms of civilizations, the recognition of local currencies could also be a sort of rehabilitation on the part of some people of the savages already colonized or being colonized. Even so western travellers and traders insisted most strongly on the fact that these odd currencies did not generally serve as intermediaries in trade relations. For the 19th and 20th Centuries Europeans who came across these societies, such goods were indeed very different from the ideal currency which is characterized by its merchant dimension and by the universality of use of one means of payment.

Therefore what was the use of these goods so precious to the local populations and whose possession might cause very intense competition between groups and individuals?

These goods, that we refer to as "paleocurrencies" rather than primitive currencies were a means of social exchange: they served to pay for births, marriages and deaths, to compensate for physical or moral injuries and breaking of taboos, to start a conflict or end one and to seal alliances. A very narrow view of this phenomena would leave you thinking that these indigenous riches were used to "buy" a wife to marry. What separates paleocurrency and modern currencies cannot be reduced to a number of different social conventions. A first step to superficially understanding the difference would be to make a list of what goods or services one or other type of currency might obtain. But an understanding of this also needs to take into account a different mental outlook on monetary reality. The paleocurrencies are not rudimentary instruments of purchase of goods such as consumer goods, tools for work or means of defence, or labor. They are much more than this for, even apart from the fact that they are a means to gain access to specific positions in society and to acquire other goods (generally without being an exact counterpart) they are living elements. They are bonds and reminders of the links existing between individuals and groups. They function as a direct instrument of control and social regulation. Also, generally there is not one single type of paleocurrency that can be sub-divided and multiplied; There is in circulation within each community or in their external relations separate series of paleocurrency and goods that act as paleocurrency which are not interchangeable and come under in hierarchical order. Each sort of goods corresponds to an obligation or specific situation. This division of uses, the differentiation in terms of age, sex. clans, casts and individuals in being able to obtain these paleocurrencies perpetuate a relationship of domination and dependency.

What similarity is there between these precious objects and our own currencies apart from the analogy of circulation? On the one hand it is possible to show that object similar to those that travellers called "primitive currencies" existed and fulfilled identical functions in ancient western societies. That coins and gold bars filled the same roles and therefore that this type of wealth can be seen as logical and historical precursors of our own currencies. Furthermore if we can grasp conceptually the monetary phenomena as a means of reducing society (above all by defining monetary practices not only in terms of payment but also with accounts and accepting that also in western society the monetary reality can not be restricted to solely the market-place) then we must agree that paleocurrencies generally have as strong a function in the monetary phenomena. It was in any case from this paleocurrency structure that "aboriginals" managed to understand how Europeans used a number system. Thus the paleocurrencies of the "savages" were considered as "primitive currencies" by the western travellers and in turn coins and notes became paleocurrencies in the eyes and in the hands of the colonized. As we will also see these instruments of payment were subverted by the thinking and customs of the "aboriginal."

"PRIMITIVE" CURRENCIES, "PALEOCURRENCIES," AND "CURRENCIES"

The Melanesians, Amerindians, Africans etc. saw the colonizers using among themselves pieces of materials (metal and then paper), which were often unknown to them until then. Yet the originality of paleocurrencies is that they are generally socially developed and arise through large craft activity or else from an extraneous source in which more or less mythical being take part. A parallel might be drawn here with the myths and tales about precious metals and the status of blacksmiths in ancient European societies. So the metal (or paper) can be seen as a magic substance which is instilled with the power of the new-comers. Their virtues might be communicated to the user. They can therefore serve as magic or religious instruments; they are passed from hand to hand to grant the benefit of their power; they are burned or submerged in water with secret chants etc. Some coins are blamed for causing pains or illnesses or the opposite as remedies that get rid of spirits or illnesses. In southern Nigeria at the start of the twentieth century only coins with the head of a living monarch were accepted by the local population. In 1945 in the New Hebrides the devaluation of the British pound was believed to be caused by the illness of the king portrayed on the coins. As with paleocurrencies it was possible that coins and banknotes be considered living elements. Coins could also to a large extent lose their monetary nature as with the Maria-Theresa thaler in East Africa which became a feminine ornament.

The second characteristic feature of western means of payment which should be considered and which might have contributed to their assimilation with paleocurrencies is that its instruments exist in standard and hierarchical series.

Finally coins and banknotes circulate backwards from goods and work of varying value. From a purely formal point of view and to those who fail to grasp more than just a part, there is no difference between an exchange of gift for another gift and buying and selling. The meaning of European transactions was misunderstood by the colonized or rather they interpreted them in a way that would have surprised the agents of these pseudo-rites. Descriptions of the cult of Cargo in Melanesia are examples of this way of thinking, as an interpretation and acting out of our monetary practices.

Thus those who were ignorant, or virtually ignorant, of the customs and practices of our financial settlements might have got the impression that coins and banknotes were the paleocurrencies of the "white man." In other words of creatures who initially might appeared as gods, or ancestors, or envoys of the gods or else simply as men from distant lands on the other side of the mountains and the seas.

This initial identification of western means of payment as paleocurrencies had very important consequences.

In their foreign relations the communities assimilated them into their own society's means of ownership and circulation, or customary channels of wealth. However when directly received from the Europeans when one became a dependent (salaried worker) or else when they were given local produce which up until then might had been ignored (such as gum) or else vegetables that the new masters introduced in farming, this (money) turned out to be the most effective means to acquire European products (clothes, furniture, food, metal, tools etc.).Products which themselves were part of a certain way of classifying things. Even today money which is obtained by the sale of some crops or by migration is often spend on specific things, while the remainder of the local economy is paid for in kind. One must also wonder how elements such as government taxes, salaries and the commercialisation of local products are experienced and understood. There might have been a variety of traditions that explained away coins or banknotes which were not obvious. The colonized saw this new development through their own eyes. In Africa for example in societies that before the colonial period did not have central governments, people who had initially given taxes could not understand why every year they had to repeat an operation which they either saw as a gift or else as the offering of the vanquished suing for peace. In Senegal the Diolas from the Lower Casamance region refused to swap rice for money, in other words to link directly rice, which was a central element in their culture, with coins and banknotes which were an element of a foreign civilisation. They exchanged measure for measure rice for peanuts (an American plant which was grown in Africa) through Mandingue traders and then sold the peanuts to pay their taxes. In Central Africa the effects of the fall in prices on the world market of raw materials on local prices was perceived by the local population as robbery since for them prices have a social relationship and not a result of the level of offer and demand.

More or less quickly the use of money extended out from the simple aboriginal-colonial relationship with an internal distribution coming about through new players on the scene. Thus the new currency were able to replace ancient paleocurrencies, or old wealth that had a paleomonetary function and as a method of social exchange which maintained one's rank within a group (matrimonial compensation, burial dues, during festivals etc.). In the Caroline islands between 1952 and 1957 the chiefs developed a cult to collect coins and banknotes in exchange for which they remitted shares of company stocks (Truck Trading Company, Mortlock Trading Company etc.). The capital collected in this way was used to buy various manufactured goods including boat engines and sewing machines, thus showing the duplicity of a seemingly religious tradition and a real integration within the world market. On occasion this substitution was not so complete: with the Pedi of Sekhukhuneland in east Africa coins and banknotes were given as dowries whereas customarily they involved heads of cattle.

The transformation of coins and notes into paleocurrency and their integration into categories of valuable goods with a rough hierarchy could produce unexpected effects. In the straits of Vitiaz, the western Pacific, the pound was considered initially as another paleocurrency, as an indivisible object. Therefore all prices were made into multiples of a pound. In other cases a local hierarchy of differing categories of coins and notes replaced their value on the international exchange (the switching of relation between copper and silver with red being considered more powerful than white) or else modifying the units of the same denomination for example with a pound being fifteen shillings instead of twenty. Where there are spheres of restricted exchange and where the various types of coins and notes have different categories then an exchange between the various monetary instruments is impossible. If these spheres have hierarchies the conversion of one unit into subdivisions requires a chain of conversion.

WHAT HAS BECOME OF THESE OLD PALEOCURRENCIES?

There was no instant distribution of western currencies. Far from metropolitan areas the settlers were few in numbers and were even forced to use improvised forms such as playing cards in North America at the end of the seventeenth century and during the eighteenth century where commercial goods were used (skins, furs, spices etc.) as currency. The colonials often had to accept in settlement for manufactured goods or taxes traditional paleocurrencies which they then redistributed in the form of salaries or for the price of local produce. The colonials did not restrict themselves, in order to increase the scope of their trade, to existing paleocurrencies. They manufactured imitations industrially: thus in Africa there were *manilles* that were a paleocurrency that was made in Europe; in New Caledonia the missionaries played a major role in the spread of imitation shells that were sold by the meter in shops. The colonials imported large numbers of cowries from the Indian ocean to Western Africa producing inflation in seashells and a major drop in their value. Counterfeits often only had limited success no doubt due to flooding the market and cheapening their value within the hierarchy of these societies and their traditional status.

The colonized with greater contact with the white man became aware that they did not generally use among themselves traditional paleocurrencies and that they did not value them elsewhere than in aboriginal settings. Western currency therefore appeared to be of real value and at the heart of the power of the colonials. Even so, apart from the problem of circulation of European currencies, these did not systematically evince the old paleocurrencies. They played the part of secondary currencies in purchases induced by the destruction of community links. When those in power no longer are able to control the means of obtaining new revenue, the relationship of dependency diminishes or is destroyed. Money again could free the younger sons who could go off to the plantations or the building sites. Coins and banknotes were therefore hermetically excluded from social obligations that are felt to be essential for the survival of the group (above all in the making of a dowry). New means of production however (above all the use of metal) might sometimes dramatically change the conditions for the production of these paleocurrencies and their form. In the Island of Yap in the Pacific, the paleocurrency was a stone disc several centimetres wide that progressively became large mill stones tens of centimetres wide. Control of the venerable paleocurrency that was needed to maintain ones rank allowed the traditional chiefs to get their hands on a large proportion of the income of those they dominated and to transform this into imported products such as alcohol, clothes, umbrellas etc. The same reasons can explain why the traditional currencies still have a residual role in ancient societies with central governments. They are used in various marriage rites and religious occasions or ceremonies of initiation while the new currencies are used for administration and trading purposes. The disappearance of the paleocurrencies is therefore dependent on the disintegration or modernisation of old relationships of domination.

We have sketched out the effects of the encounter between cultures that consider money in very different ways. Thus in a sort of speeding up of history the paleocurrencies have become currencies and currencies reverting to their old roles have become paleocurrencies. Even so, each culture perceived only a fraction of the other; outlandish practices were rationalized and sometimes behavior that seemed impossible to imitate became a source of puzzlement. Thus Touiavii, a Tiaera chief in the South Pacific who was brought to Germany at the start of the twentieth century, reported in his speech to the members of his tribe on his return some astounding findings. Touiavii said: "Many white men get money earned for them by others, place it in a well-guarded place, always take more until the day when they no longer need others to work for them since the money works in their stead." He added: "I never managed to find out how this was possible without black-magic, although this is the way it happens, money multiplies itself like the leaves on a tree and the man becomes richer even while he is sleeping."

TRAVELS OF MONEY

Erik Orsenna

I was surprised to find that I had so many links with money.... I shall be content here to sketch four very different points. The first is my thesis, a "bestseller" at 323 copies, called *Espace national et desequilibre monetaire* ("The Nation and Monetary Disequilibrium") with 800 pages on item 383 of the balance of payments. Then the rather extraordinary and unexpected experience, if truth be told, that I had with the Goncourt prize. Thirdly my work as a public servant. Finally the Third World.

Firstly the thesis. At the time I was studying economics I was a member of the PSU (United Socialist Party). Full of confidence, I thought that one day the left would finally win, which is what happened, as you probably know. I told myself: "If the left wins, no doubt there will be a lot of speculative movement of money. So there it will be useful to have some left-wingers who know how to stop these speculative transfers. Therefore let us study the balance of payments."

I had a pretty good understanding of the balance of payments. Yet I had not understood an essential feature of French society: I had not studied at ENA (National Economic Institute). Even if I had studied at ENA, I was not an inspector of finance. Whether the left or the right win nobody but inspectors of finance would have any influence in the matter of money. Therefore when the left did win, I was told in no uncertain terms that I need not busy myself with the fight against speculation.

They told me: "You take care of cocoa." So I worked on raw materials and above all cocoa, and with great zest. I had just moved to my offices near that of Jean-Pierre Cot, minister for cooperation. The telephone rang. Our representative in Brussels was on the line: "Counsellor, there is a cocoa crisis! We have over-run our quota. What should we do?" I had been a teacher. Now I had to act. How thrilling!

Another event occurred a few years later: the Goncourt prize. An hour after the announcement, I was handed a telegram that began with "bravo!" then followed five lines of thanks. It came from the Minister for the Budget, Mr. Charasse. It meant: "Bravo for the prize" and thanks for the income tax that I was going to pay him. It is interesting to see what a literary prize means in terms of money. The amount of the Goncourt is enormous; no salary can match it. In terms of property it is "only" 120 to a flat of 150 square meters in Paris.

At the Lyon book fair Paul-Lou Sulitzer came towards me and said: "Congratulations, old man!" Imagine how you feel when a best-selling author comes to you and congratulates you. Then he drew me aside and said: "Now for the real work: you will have to start managing your finances!" This was one of the highlights of these days.

The experience of the world of film-making, following the award was rather different. You meet someone for lunch, since these things can only be clinched over lunch. It happened to be Regis Wargnier who was working on a project for the film *Indochine* and the financial rewards were considerably above what you can earn with books.

In planning a scene for a film, one has to think of the budget, unless you are irresponsible, and of the time-table since it is an industry. Literature is quite the opposite, it is all about taking your time, waiting, being carried along. In the process of writing, whether it is a book or a scenario, there are different paces. The relationship with time and money varies and passing from one to the other needs the skill of an acrobat at times.

Thirdly, my experience in the public service as an advisor. You are between 30 and 35 years old. You earn about 20,000 francs a month. At the moment I am an advisor to Mr. Dumas (the Foreign Minister. All in all, including bonuses, I make 24,000 francs. I am a ministerial advisor in charge of all relations with southern Europe and the whole of North Africa. Every second or third months I receive an offer from the private sector for 60-80,000 francs. What do I do? Some leave, others stay. Most of us leave. In the United States careers are different. Many work for the state for a while, later they go off to earn a bit of money and then come back. There is a sort of swing to and fro. Pay is an urgent problem in the civil service which remains to be settled.

Fourthly, the Third World. Exactly ten years ago, almost to the day, I was at Cancun. Cancun, I would remind those who are young, was a sort of grand gathering of 22 heads of state when speeches were made that have not been followed by action, such as: "A global New Deal: we will give money to everybody, etc." There was a feeling of guilt, the wish to support the third world and even a form of Third Worldism. Ten years later, dealing directly with these problems, I notice that we no longer say "guilt" but "efficiency"; we no longer say "global" but "regional."

I will only mention three points. First, the debt: today the south pays more to the north than it receives.

Second, the idea of development. Everybody knows that aid is essential but it is not with so-called public money that development can be effected. The only form of development is linked to investment and depends on enterprise. What is investment? Confidence. And confidence comes from a belief in the locals' time and investment. When no private citizen invests his own money into his country and when heads of state, especially the African ones, deposit money creamed from their country into Swiss accounts, then one starts to wonder what is the use of international aid.

Thirdly: the limits of a free market economy. What does the north ask for, discreetly but insistently? Drugs. On the same day that the USA refused to prop up coffee prices, which lost Columbia 1 billion dollars, they proposed to support their war against drugs with a maximum outlay of 200 million dollars. Let us not forget that today no part of the planet can stand in isolation.

These are some of the financial circuits of today, their interdependency and my contribution to the list of the most obvious inconsistencies in modern society.

SOME PHILOSOPHIC THOUGHTS ON MONEY

Michel Henry

Why should we think about money from the point of view of philosophy? Is money not an economic factor and therefore the business of economists—a science that they elucidate and like all branches of contemporary science has taken giant strides recently, to such an extent that only specialists can speak about the contents of their field.

To philosophize about money is only really possible or necessary on condition that money is not solely or essentially an economic factor, but arises from an origin with a different focus, heterogeneous with economics and more ancient. Since its genesis was transcendental (in other words creative) then an understanding of what money in fact is also stems from this genesis, and begs the question: what part of the origins of money is not economic.

That money does not exist by itself can be understood simply by considering that in nature, where man needed to survive, there are stones, earth, water, vegetation but no money—no more than triangles or circles. In the same way that triangles and circles are a product of thought, invented through a proto-founding process (phenomenologists would call it a transcendental birth) so too with money; even though the proto-founding act that produced it and continues to produce it continually, is different from the inspired intellectual process of abstraction that gave birth to geometry.

To sketch out the genesis of money, I will fall back on a philosopher, since he was the only one who grasped it, Karl Marx. Such a statement might seem strange nowadays at a time when all the regimes that were built up on the principles of Marxist theory are disintegrating, emphasizing their complete and utter failure. I would refute this objection by stating that Marx's thinking has nothing to do with Marxism. It systematically contradicts it and makes for the most comprehensive critique imaginable.

How and by what means was money born, that is to say created as money and continually produced and reproduced as such? It arises from the process of life, not in a biological molecular sense, but life as we know it, through actual sensation, action, suffering and fulfillment. This life that according to Marx has five characteristics: it is subjective, personal, mainly active because basically responding to need, and when need turns into anguish it changes into action which aims to satisfy it. Finally life exists in a universe that it continuously seeks to change in order to satisfy the demands of its desires.

This continual transformation of the universe through the subjective praxis of living people, which is at the root of history and society, Marx saw as the very process of establishing objects of practical value, which in itself is anything but economic. Yet the more this process developed the more the ensuing objects of practical value became diversified and numerous, the more the exchange of these becomes a problem to be solved. How does one exchange totally different objects and in what proportion? This exchange of objects of practical value is dependent on the labor that goes into making them. To set the proportion according to which such an object of practical value might be exchanged—its exchange value—involves measuring the actual work that went into its production.

Yet this elegant solution of classical economics seemed to Marx as a philosopher to be a fallacy. In his eyes work being subjective in a strict sense, being invisible, eludes any objective reckoning, either qualitative or quantitative. It is impossible to measure it. This difficulty was pushed to the limit in the *Critique of the German Workers' Party programme* with its examination of the communist principle which is seen as a principle of justice and equality with each receiving according to his labor. However, since this labor is subjective, invisible, unquantifiable, varies from one individual to the next according to his strength and individual capabilities. It follows that the effort and difficulty that one individual might have in doing the same task could be much greater than for someone other. To give the same pay or social reward for plainly different individual actions is clearly unjust. To consider every person as a worker, as communism does (capitalism also) is to carry to the limit differences of talent and gifts, is the ultimate injustice. "Equal rights," writes Marx succinctly, "means an inegalitarian right for unequal labor."

The proto-founding act of the economy aims to make exchange possible despite the enormous difference between subjects and hence actual labour. To overcome this gulf of subjectivity a crucial substitution was performed—the replacement of the invisible, individual and subjective actual labor by something objective that is held as equivalent to that labour which, since it is objective, might be perceived objectively. This equivalent to actual labour, buried in the obscurity of its deepest subjectivity is the same work but "in reverse." In other words seen as a representation, brought to light and observable. In this representation of labor as something outside itself, it in effect becomes a visible entity which can be named (saying "work"), qualified (as hard work), an objective kind of labor fixed in time and that can be measured(for example 8 hours). In this representation outside the person in the real world, work is emptied of its subjective phenomenological content which made it a living, inescapably individual reality—to become unreal, general, social, abstract, ideal, qualified and quantified. This is "work" that economists write about.

Yet it is this objectively qualified and quantified labor projected onto the product of real work (objects of practical value) that creates it exchange value. The exchange value is in the reflection in the product of the work that went into it. There is an identity between the exchange value and the work it represents—both have the same importance, the same composition and the same reality. This substance is the denial of ingredients, it is insubstantial; this reality is the denial of all that, in Marx's eyes, makes up reality, or the reality of the world and more precisely that of a subjectivity which as a praxis holds this universe in its grip and snatches it all the time from nothingness.

The same status of exchange value and labor in abstract, in other words, the work of economists, is however the status granted to the general economic reality, since all economic definition is the variation on this labor and this exchange value. So the "economic reality" is basically unreal, it is a generality, an ideal, an abstraction, or as Marx himself wrote an "alienation" but not in the Hegelian meaning of the word. An abstraction or alienation because in this exteriorising the palpable subjectivity of the initial work has lost all the elements that arise with subjectivity: suffering, pain, intensity of effort—in short everything that is a living experience is excluded. To hold as Marxists and economists in general do that the economy is at the heart of reality and therefore of society is from Marx's point of view, the most ridiculous possible statement. The economy is not real but is a distorted mirror image.

The exchange value is what labor represents in the product which once invested by this representation becomes a merchandise.

Yet this notion of work, rather than being invested into the product/ merchandise might be perceived as such, that is to say separate from the material substance of the merchandise. Money is therefore the unadulterated support of exchange value. Yet, whether the representation of labour is embodied in the goods or perceived in its pure state in money, in any case this representation is dual, it is the notion of a representation, it represents the social, abstract, general work of economists, which is an abstraction compared to the real world of work. In economic life, human activity which is the only effective force, has become a work-object, which itself is represented in its pure form by money-object. This is the transcendental genesis of money.

From this genesis, money exhibits the various characteristics which can be observed and therefore the role it has in the economic field. Its nature: an ideal objectivity or the notion of labour. Yet the exchange value is itself derived from the notion of labor and work itself, the abstract work of economists, is the representation of living labor. This means, as the transcendental genesis of money showed, that money, exchange value and labor are largely homogenous. Theoretically the genesis of money is absolutely the same as the general economic reality. In practice, the substantial homogeneity of money, exchange values and work explains why they can be exchanged all the time one against the other. In principle a metamorphosis of all economic determinants is possible within one another. Let us take the most simple exchange: 40 francs worth of tea is exchanged for 40 francs which in turn are exchanged for 40 francs worth of coffee. In this exchange there is the same amount of abstract labor that appears in three different ways: a certain amount of tea, money in its pure form and a certain amount of coffee. It is the abstract nature of money, its lack of regard as to the material expression of merchandise, that permits it to be present either in the form of tea or coffee, or else in its pure form as money. It is due to the abstract nature of labor that a flow of merchandise is possible and they can be exchanged ad infinitum.

There is a contradiction in the notion of the market economy stemming from the nature of money. The abstract nature of money allows it to be present in every form of merchandise in terms of their value and so allow for exchange. Yet the same abstract nature of money permits it to withdraw from the merchandise into its pure form as money. This is what happens in the course of every sale.

Money is a third party in relation to the merchandise, a reality independent of the goods which must face up to it. The possibility of exchanging the goods due to its specific value becomes exterior when it appears as money: the exchange, the sale of the goods becomes contingent in relation to itself. A crisis is implicit in the market economy due to its very possibility. This constant possibility of a crisis is a reality in capitalism in so far as it does not aim at producing goods but money and that the production of goods is just a means to obtain money through their sale. Therefore they it is imperative to sell immediately, yet this necessity is faced with the contingency of selling, or the independence of money in relation to the product, which in itself shows the independence of the exchange value as opposed to the practical value. This in turn shows the independence of the social element as opposed to the real experience of labor and their separate existence which is no other than the transcendental genesis of money and of the economy in general.

The abstraction of money, the fact that it can be removed from what the goods are made of and can exist on its own, appears to give it a life of its own. In this autonomous existence money could have its own laws, its own future and its means of action. The world in which money has its very own value is where it would be totally independent—where money sets its own value and will change into more money. Thus money earns interest, a profit, an income, there are rates of interest, profit rates, etc.

This autonomy of money is an appearance, an illusion which belies its abstract nature, the fact that, as pure fiction and an ideal reality, money can only survive when it is based on a reality of another kind that creates it continuously and without which it would disappear. Marx interpreted this dependence of money in three ways: its inability to grow by itself or more precisely the impossibility of capital unless as a consequence of the exploitation of people, its inability to maintain itself because of the impossibility of maintaining the practical values of commodities in which the capital is invested and thus the constant involvement of real work, and finally its inability to exist simply as money since its existence is none other than a representation of actual labor. The reality outside of which economic reality does not exist is therefore real life. This is why all the analyses made by Marx have one objective: to establish that when money or capital seem to achieve something in fact this is not true. Money has to be converted into a living force, to buy labor or as

Marx saw it a person. Far from being independent, capital is constantly invested. To understand its history, the risks involved, one has to stand "outside the market-place," "leave this noisy sphere where everything is surface-deep and obvious" and look under "into the secret laboratory of production" at the heart of subjectivity which strives to create practical added values and thus exchange values which are in principle representations that fall short of this effort. Or, as Marx said once, see "not only how capital produces but also how it is produced."

Nowadays are these analyses—the reference of money to life—out of date? If one looks towards the east, one finds in the fall of the communist regimes a strong confirmation of Marx's theory in that when individuals are idle everything grinds to a halt. Nor will society replace them since in Marx's mind society does not exist. What about looking at the west? In the west we see what is progressively replacing the individual: Galilean modern technology. Human labor is progressively being excluded from the actual process of production of practical added values in favor of objective processes. If human labor is the only thing that gives value or money then the latter will tend to disappear at the same time as labor. What today is seen as an ideal solution—the market forces—is precisely what will become a problem. How is it possible to base the production of increasing tangential practical added values on exchange values that are becoming extinct? I should have called this short paper "The Decline of Money."

Whatever the fate of money, it is still present with all its mystery. To think philosophically about money does not mean to resolve this mystery but on the contrary to acknowledge it since it is part of life. In the *1844 Manuscripts*, "young" Marx quoted Shakespeare who said that gold is "mankind's common whore." Yet on the oldest worn-out coins, on the dirtiest bank-notes there appears, perhaps indistinctly, the figure of a man.

MONEY ON A UNIVERSAL SCALE ACCORDING TO GEORG SIMMEL

Jean-Louis Vieillard-Baron

Georg Simmel was a German philosopher who lived from 1858 to 1918. He was a friend of Bergson and Rodin and was greatly affected by the First World War. He was a well-known Berlin figure who was hated by contemporary orthodox academics. He never managed to get a chair as professor of philosophy at Berlin University and it was only when he was 55 that he obtained the little-coveted chair at Strasbourg University that in 1914 had been German since 1871. What did they blame him for? Above all for his freedom of thought. In the words for thinking rather than working, for having a critical mind rather than pointless erudition. Of course his German muse did not know either Latin or Greek. He was deeply interested in modernity.

This might explain why he wrote a weighty *Philosophy of Money* that has recently been translated into French. The title is provoking. Is not an intellectual above money matters? If money only serves to satisfy desires, is not the intellectual someone whose ideas are or claim to be completely independent of desires? Was not philosophising about money something unworthy and too temporal? Should not the aim to break with the narcissistic pleasures to dwell in the world of ideas and avoid the degrading proximity of the reality of everyday experience? It was a strange novelty to want to thus write a "philosophie" of money; no philosopher had done so before nor since.

The left-wing intellectual dislikes talk of money; this can be seen by the problems that university unions have in prioritizing demands for salaries. The problem of wages is seen as appropriate for the school teachers unions while the university unions are more interested in the "corridors of power," in the pleasures of strolling in ministers' corridors to glean the notorious "corridor rumours" and eventually influence such and such a decision. Hence "power" is a noble aspiration, while "money" is a shameful aspiration. This is gradually changing since the left-wing intellectual is no longer a valuable commodity; however rarity might once more make it an asset.

The subject of money was taboo among the bourgeoisie of the nineteenth century; it was totally inconceivable to mention the price of things, much less one's income. On this question agreement seems to have had important ethical reasons and Marx is a good example. I will quote a short passage of the pages dealing with money from the *1844 Manuscript* in which a virtuous criticism of money was expressed in the most intellectual, bourgeois and moralizing way possible: "Money is the widespread perversion of what makes an individual which it changes into his opposite by giving him qualities which are not at all his."

It thus seems to be a force of corruption in the individual, in social relations etc. that seem essential. It changes fidelity into infidelity, love into hate, hate into love, virtue into vice, vice into virtue, the valet into the master, stupidity into intelligence and intelligence into stupidity.

Money as the notion of value with real influence, confuses and makes everything interchangeable; through it everything can be converted. It turns the world upside down, transforming and confusing all natural human qualities."

What Marx expresses is the archetypal intellectual attitude of the nineteenth century with money as the corrupter; as a means of exchange it muddles roles and pervert values, the highest being that of intelligence into stupidity—which was very clear for an intellectual who puts ideas at the summit of his hierarchy of values.

Georg Simmel's analysis of money is the exact opposite of Marx's. Firstly, money is the most neutral reality there is; it is a mechanism totally independent of what it prices. An exchange creates a sort of objective evaluation of reality. Where there is no exchange, the evaluation remains purely subjective. Theft and gift are types of appropriation and transfer that precede exchange; they only express subjective impulses. I covet a beautiful motorbike, and steal it; I love a woman and give her a diamond. There is no exchange since an exchange presupposes an objective pricing, thought, mutual agreement and restraint of momentary envy. Formally the process of exchange is relatively fair. Only an exchange that goes through the channel of money can provide a relatively equal satisfaction to both parties. He who buys receives exactly what he needs and he who sells gets money or in other words what everybody needs. A nostalgic primitivism or a disenchanted need for exoticism is behind the many studies that some of our contemporaries have made on the subject of barter, which is exchange without money. Levi-Strauss helpfully remarked that when we dream of the Bororo or African village, or Melanesian forms of barter etc. we should never forget that these societies were profoundly in decline. Money however is a sign of modernity.

Simmel was criticized for being too interested in modern society, in huge urban landscapes such as New York and for having ignored important values. Yet when one reads him one notes above all a desire for close analysis and reluctance to jump to conclusions. Hence why he was able to make a "philosophy of money" while at the same time being interested in the most disinterested of art forms, in mysticism and metaphysics.

Simmel said that money was an "ordinary means." The frightened and romantic critics of money based their argument on the confusion between money itself and the wish to possess it or cupidity which are vices that could arise both in a monetary economy as well as in a non monetary economy. Money and property are not the same.

Starting from this angle, there are two sorts of possible comments:

- money is a symbol of the modern tendency to reduce qualitative criteria to quantitative ones.
- money is a factor of the modern tendency to impart more objectivity and more meaning into human behavior.

Simmel's thoughts on money seem to me to be both lucid and prophetic as he anticipated various social realities which have only appeared in the last two decades.

Let us first turn to the first point: money is the symbol of the modern tendency to stress the quantitative factor. Simmel does not argue over this point; he makes no attempt to show in a metaphysical way that quality is a the bottom of quantity and how following Bergson's line of thought "due to the quality of quantity we are able to conceive quantity without quality."

The reducing of quality to a number of quantifiable factors is obvious, even in history, where minor social phenomena are studied rather than the actions of heroic individuals; and even when we recognize the overpowering importance of a few individuals these tend to be explained by reference to collective factors. This democratic tendency is embedded deep inside the psychological landscape and it is said that what matters is not the achievement of a moment but the everyday life. Modern thought attempts to understand systematically specifics, the individual, the qualitative by a varying construct of quantifiable elements. In this sense Nietzsche was not a modern author: he felt that only the quality of man was important; the value of an epoch was only measured by the above-average men who lived in it. This aristocratic attitude rejects the importance of the relative spread of values and states of being that are aspired to.

Two comments can be made about the constant progress of quantitative evaluation through money. A historian might be under the "illusion" that variations in the price of corn in the twelfth century were more important than the thoughts of Saint Bernard; yet this would be forgetting that human existence alternates (as emphasized by Simmel in other essays) between the everyday—which need not always be denigrated—and adventure where the creative individual takes on another dimension. Secondly that the modern tendency is to "see money as a central and absolute value" whereas it is only a means. Simmel felt, better than many that followed, that this modernity of ours gave precedence to an individual mobility of means. Nothing is so handy than money, for the individual; similarly the remarkable achievements of technology; what is essential are things that can follow the individual around and fulfill several purposes. Yet when their numbers increase then they end up being less valuable, since people measure the qualitative value of something in terms of their price.

Whatever the negative effects of the increasing importance of money in our lives, Simmel observed and analyzed the causes, however he radically freed the analysis of money from the obvious question of pleasure. His study restored money to the evolution of social interaction but it kept in mind the fact that modern man is not solely an "economic factor," but that psychologically and intellectually "entered the economic life."

Let us come to the second point:

> Objectivity in the typical human behavior of give and finds its most complete expression in purely monetary and economic deals. [...] Money thus removes human subjectivity from various actions or human relations in the same way that inner thought, when it is purely intellectual, breaks with personal subjectivity and becomes part of the objective order which it reflects....

But a counter argument immediately arises against the objectivity of the correlation intellect and monetary economy:

> Together with this impersonal objectivity which is an attribute of intelligence because of its range of activity, there exists a very close link between this intelligence on the one hand, and on the other hand, the individual personality and everything that goes with individualism. Even though in its own way money transforms the impulsive and subjective process into objective and supra-personal norms, it is no less an arena for the individualism and economic egotism to flourish.

Here was one of Simmel's most important achievements to have shown that the raising of the general level of culture, and general advances in knowledge "would not result in a general leveling of society but quite the contrary." In reality money is apparently an objective measure of everything quantifiable. But it is the individual culture which results in its good or ill-advised use. Accepting that ability is not socially or adequately rewarded in terms of pay, the superiority of a cultured man over one who is not will always remain. For one can share money but one cannot share culture apart from very superficially. One could teach everyone exactly the same—at least theoretically according to the republican ideal bequeathed by Jules Ferry—yet one could never ensure that everyone receives this learning in the same way. It is only by individual effort that culture, which is generally open to all, becomes a real part of the individual and reveals who truly is a cultured person.

Seen as a cultural factor, money bears witness to the dual tendency of modern culture. Objectively it is everything that is produced in every field; the enlargement of scientific knowledge means that it is way over the head of the individual and that it has become specialized—in a similar way knowledge of monetary processes gives a specialized knowledge even though it is uncertain. Subjective knowledge means the body of knowledge a person may have received through education but also of another order, such as social skills, through other channels. Yet modern times are characterized by the growing gap between objective culture and the perforce limited chances that a person has of becoming cultured. The use of money by the individual would therefore become increasingly varied and also difficult.

The task of a philosophy of money of which Simmel gave an excellent example seems to me to be that of a philosophy of the spirit of objectivity. Hegel felt that the objective spirit was everything that humans did in order to create institutions. It was once believed that sociology and ethnology could study the social behavior of man and empirically tell us about the truth of human life rather than speculating about it. However I believe that sociology has become the "ideology of our age" in the sense that everyone sees the basic problems of humanity from a social angle. Yet this ideological function of sociology should in itself be questioned. Philosophy is not hostile to the essential idea of a social force however it can not weakly accept its predominance. The temptation of sloppy thinking is to reduce every problem to their social dimension and ignore the various levels of reality in which people are involved. A philosophy of objective thought shows how human institutions are not self-sufficient. Money is not a separate element but is part of life and emphasizes a *social model* just as mathematics apply to an *intellectual model*. Yet the way in which each person aspires to these models varies from individual to individual. It is here that Simmel always points out the continual interaction of the individual and society. Bergson said that society is in the individual as much as the individual is in society. Philosophy is always the thoughts of the individual about himself even when they aim to be purely universal. It cannot take refuge in the world of pure ideas. The understanding of the universal role of money in society raises the question of the values that may govern its use.

Money is not a superficial question for philosophy; it is as important as the daily experience of man. The denigration of the everyday is as absurd as reducing man to the level ants and seeing us only as social beings. The dimension of exchange that is manifested and developed with money is also found at the psychological level of subjective thought. Without exchange man is doomed, from every conceivable point of view. But money depersonalizes our relation to things. Is this a pity? It seems to me that on the contrary this can result in a broadening of man's horizons. Our present way of thinking no longer allows us to believe in the immutability of objects. Individual freedom can only gain from this, the only true constants being in terms of people and transcendental values.

I have studied mysticism closely enough not to feel that this is a marginal or odd concept. The poetic experience, and artistic experience in general as the metaphysical experience are related to the mystical experience. They are a sublimation of man, searching for his own image under the gaze of the Absolute. Yet these experiences find a meaning only in opposition to daily life. The study of daily life is not too mean a task for the philosopher. On the contrary, it shows, in a way that is hard and unexciting, how the attitude of man to money reflects the most profound currents in the evolution of ideas and of the soul. What has to be avoided is a confusion of levels of reality, for economic mysticism is as dangerous as intellectuals in government. In reality, there are only two recent philosophers, Hegel and Bergerson, who have cast any light on the distinction between these levels and their connection, in such a way that we can understand how a strange creature such as man, who is capable of the highest mystical experience is at the same time able to express his freedom in relation to money. They have avoided the trap of empty sophistication that contemporary philosophical currents often fall into and retained as the essential view of philosophy that man has to be considered in his entirety.

MONEY AS ALIBI

Alain Cotta

This seminar is intended to answer the question: "How should we think of money?" I was struck at first by the provocation it contained. We are trained to distinguish between three levels of education, the primary one dealing with "what" contents, the secondary applying to the "how" and higher education being more concerned with "why." Hence the title of this conference might imply there is no need to think of money in any other way but the secondary one, and wonder whether it is necessary to do so. But obviously one cannot study the various ways without a clear idea of the reason why. We might otherwise run the risk of pursuing blindly an area of scientific research which like all others needs clear thinking on human behavior.

As soon as this line of reasoning opens up, we come against a paradox which I should explain seeing that it indicates the reason for not limiting ourselves to "thinking of money." This does not mean that money does not exist, and R. Lion proved it decisively, nor does it contradict my colleague Guillaume's assertions as to its various forms. Of course money does exist, under various guises, it follows certain channels and procedures, it enjoys powers and many men and women make a career of it, all the signs are there to show that it exists. However, should we reflect on it?

Whatever its forms, whatever its powers, whatever the procedures of financial activity, money fulfills an essential social function owing to three characteristics. In the first place, it is a unit of measure, a yardstick. In this respect it can be defined less as a convention than a token of trust. Money expresses two basic kinds of trust: on the one hand, it makes exchanges possible and all the mechanics of economic socialization depends on it and on the other hand, it helps in moving up the social ladder. However strong the above mentioned convention and the two relations of trust which condition it are, there should be no mental apprehension of money, this is not enough.

Let us first examine the convention; in reality, when we say: "one franc, two francs" we give an estimate; in short, money is the only social yardstick at our disposal. This question has been discussed at length in the course of this conference, as it lies at the heart of a debate which started with the industrial revolution. Controversies arose over the connection between money taken as a method of accounting, the intrinsic value of something and above all its price. Does the price of a property, of a human being, of whatever, as expressed in terms of money, reflect its "value"? This debate which has been going on for two centuries is now largely meaningless and we should not wonder at this.

From the very beginning, going back to Aristotle, it was a debate in which "the theory of money" provided an alibi. We know why it was felt to be necessary. We had to proclaim, for two centuries: "Of course, money does not correspond with value. Price is no indication of value." I fully realize that the distinction between the terms value and valorization became blurred intentionally. Yet the theory of money as a measuring system provided an alibi making it possible to assert that the price of something did not coincide with its value, therefore there had to be another yardstick, for example the notion of work involved in it.

It is probably this basic principle of the Marxist ideology which has come under the most violent attack in the last ten years. This is not to say that Marx no longer matters: it would take a singularly inexperienced person or a blind fanatic to assert that, because some wretched people's commissars made a mess of his theories, that have become irrelevant. Still the demise of the Soviet economy, of centralized planning, the zeal shown by French socialist ministers in helping to set into motion a market economy in the ex-Soviet Union, is proof that money as a conventional power has won the day. It is likely that for a long time there will be no arguing about value and price, valorization and price, because it will remain obvious that price, as expressed in monetary terms, may not be the only social convention available but that it is the most convenient to live with.

From this point of view, the alibi provided by money was a mere diversion on the stage. Its role was minimal and is no longer needed as the function of money as a yardstick has lost any relevance.

On the contrary, money is still very much present in the two areas of trust it is endowed with. First of all in the process of exchange where it expresses the "purchasing power" of our income. Leon Bloy gave a splendid definition of money: "Money is freedom in the shape of currency." In other words, our freedom can be measured, whether we like it or not, by the level of income whose variations from one person to another are the basis of social inequalities. Our incomes show wide differences and put a limit to our spending levels. Hence the importance we attach to money, to the monetary evaluation of our income and its use in attacking an injustice that we feel we suffer from. All the people with a low income (that is a large majority), in the comparative and absolute sense, are concerned with money. "How unfair is our lot in life!" As for the others, according to their culture, civilization and the country they happen to live in, they speak but little of their high income or they may derive from it a belief in their intrinsic superiority.

Thus the consciousness of the inequalities between the economic capability of the people who coexist in a community or society is embodied in the level of individual incomes. If, besides, we assert that feelings and, above all, life itself are, as we saw earlier, in a category where estimates are not relevant, we set a partition between goods and the rest, what can be assessed in terms of money and all other things, more or less noble, which lie outside its range.

This attitude amounts to an alibi which in itself may do great harm to our personal destinies. We should be careful not to dwell on this conception of inequalities, even though it is an effective rallying cry. We should not think in these terms either of our lives or other people's. Inequalities in incomes can be traced to specific reasons, birth, social position, physical and intellectual abilities, character. There is an intellectual inequality which prevents 30% of an age group of acquiring the lowest school qualification. It is such an evident drawback that desperate efforts are being made to draw so-called unqualified people into the social set-up through purely financial means. In short, income discrepancies, inequalities in our personal and social circumstances reflect much deeper phenomena which are not related only to social position but also with natural or biological dispositions. Refusing to recognize this fact can only lead to wishful thinking and ineffectual policies. On the other hand, when we say life is "priceless" we draw on feelings and neglect the evidence of reason. Life is always given a new value; it has a price which varies according to each historical period and each society. Some societies succeed in preserving the life of their members because they are able to give it an objective price, while others, less developed, cannot manage this.

Whatever our moral objections to this assertion, the life of the former is worth more than the latter's. Can we and should we keep apart the second world as defined by Popper from his primitive one made up of inert matter and money? Should we give a monetary value to the non-marketable by acknowledging the truth of the saying which holds that nothing will cost so much a man as a woman who loves him for his own sake, or of the proverb "No money, no Swiss guards"? We have long been aware that the weight, consequences and effects of our feelings have a cost, though we do our utmost to conceal the fact, if only to legitimize our deep-felt affections.

Thus whatever the stand we take, whether money serves to buy and sell or only to give a value to our passions, it is little more than a screen. What could be hidden behind it, except our condition in relation to that of other people, our social situation, our place on the hierarchical ladder which depends as much on the most individual and transitory factors as on universal and permanent ones. Concentrating on money, neglecting other aspects of our circumstances, our biological assets and position in society, shows serious lack of judgment and a warped apprehension of reality.

Money also implies another kind of trust which is essential to our capacity as an individual or a group to accumulate and represents the basic requirement for any economic and social development. Thus it is possible to create wealth out of money from an initial deposit. Money insofar as it is linked with wealth constitutes a means of exchange; insofar as it is linked with wealth, money reflects a sustained effort and layers of savings carried out over several generations possibly. But even then, when we think of money, what attitude do we adopt? We assume that someone's wealth is a sign of success, the manifestation of his capacity to gain and mobilize at will a certain power. It is also widely held that a person's wealth bears testimony to his love for his children, or even that money is the result of a transfer and a substitute for sexual relations as psychoanalysts would have us believe.

This is quite rational, money being the main agent in the building of capital. Yet one should pursue the matter further. In reality, we all know that money, for all our talk about the next generation, and whether we enjoy the material aspect of it or not, as we grow older and this explains the phenomenon of miserliness among the old, fundamentally represents a pitiful means of exorcising death. Money becomes more and more like death as it grows increasingly remote from life. Our savings banks, supposed to be as safe as houses, would not mind offering a safe haven against risks of any kinds, including mortality. For the time being they content themselves with an interest rate, but who knows, they may turn to religion? Robert Lion would enjoy unprecedented success if he tried to sell eternal peace in reasonable comfort.

Thus if we try to think of money, each one of us, some will take it as a means of exchange while others see it as income or wealth, we artificially freeze it. Its impact on society and the search for ways of improving its role is thus distorted. Contrary to appearances, excessive concern for money leads to passive resignation rather than frenzied activity.

It may be futile to examine the contents of the notion of money, we should rather wonder why it exists, why we use it and wish to acquire more, why it is a symbolic gesture to burn a bank-note, why most of us would not dream of doing it, why we try to hang on to money even if we should feel ashamed of the means to achieve this.

It must be acknowledged that money is a kind of artifact which enables men to live together within these huge communities of comparatively recent emergence that are called nations and perhaps tomorrow in a wider body, the human species. We have to recognize the fact that money has nothing to do with culture in the sense Michel Serres gives to the word, that is to say a way of living rather than an exclusive kind of erudition dependent on fashions. Culture has nothing to do with money, but rests on three bases, all related to our attitude to the body and to the French essentially food, to sex and to death. Money in this triple configuration is nothing more than a commodity which, if we understand it as we are asked to do in this conference, that is to say if we look for "the reason for its being there," makes us disorientated, prevents our understanding of social inequalities as caused by conditions easy enough to identify, such as the fact that we were born in one place rather than another, with neurological assets or not, in a certain relation to power, *hic* and *nunc* rather than elsewhere.

We would be gravely mistaken therefore to dwell on a fixed picture of money which would lead us to believe that we are not fully responsible for our circumstances and our behavior and that on this assumption a neutral power exerts its influence through the effects of a higher or lower interest rate, and a more or less rigid monetary or financial policy.

In any case, money is more than an alibi. It sends back a flattering image of our ego. It acts as intermediary between it and death. Modern society gives much importance to money and, if we are content with reflecting on its meaning, we turn our backs on all hope of moral improvement and clear-sightedness. Our great poet, Rene Char once said: "Lucidity is the wound in us that is closest to the sun." It is unlikely that a close look at money may preserve us from the wound he ardently prayed for.

The Principles of Pricelessness

Jacques Derrida

The key word today is the need to economize and to make reductions, above all regarding time. Let us examine the words of the title as suggested at the first meeting, which seems to me entirely suitable: the spirit of the market. Should the expression be taken literally, as the spirit is often in opposition with the letter?

It could be argued that under the name of money the spirit of the market should be contrasted with its letter, that is to say the wording of the exchanges, the physical element of the monetary reality, which can be measured, recorded and translated into numbers. The spirit of the market would then refer, among other things, to everything that, under the name of money, does not belong to the economic sphere. Money as spirit of the market would be the part of an exchange which either does not belong strictly to the economy as seen in a narrow sense, and cannot be encompassed in a theoretical framework, through numbers and objective criteria, or is a part which, still belonging to the economic order, which goes beyond auditing material goods, commercial exchanges or the production of commodities.

In both cases, the spirit of the market would apply, at least in the area of difficulties that might arise, to a set of rules, motives and ends underlying the commercial system without being part of it. This determining element could be contained in money, either as a non-economical value, or money as an economic value of a higher kind, outside the range of currency. Money can then be said to be more and less than its cash equivalent.

In both instances, the element of accountability seems to be overshadowed by the immaterial and irrational power of what we call "money," as distinct from ready cash, providing such a distinction is relevant. The present conference has elected to concentrate on what lies outside the strictly monetary, taking for granted that the notion of currency emerged at a later date than the notion of money, and its history comparatively independent, and that a scientific approach can be appropriate to currency as separate from money or economic value.

Again let us repeat that only conventional wisdom in certain circumstances makes a distinction between currency and money.

First two observations need to be made. Both words or concepts, money and currency, apply to something that is not to be found in nature. They both depend on what credit attaches to conventions, technical devices and regulations. Even before the development of credit mechanisms and fiduciary arrangements, they were both (money just as much as currency) manifestations of the phenomenon of credit as governed by conventions, they had ceased to belong to what is usually called the natural world to come into the symbolic realm of "*fides publica*," which implies trust into a solemn oath. They oblige us to face the enigma of the odd and familiar experience of "belief," the treasure-trove of philosophers. What I wish to bring to the fore rests on the age-old distinction between nature and convention, nature and the law, nature and art or technique, a fundamental and historical opposition whose background it would be fascinating but beyond the time limit imparted to us to study. Suffice it to say that the notions of exchange or economic production, of value or goods, of money or currency, are more than one example of this opposition. There is neither history, nor convention, art or technique without production, distribution of labor, or without the emergence of an exchange value and currency. In an attempt to resist the common tendency to view the history of currency or economic value as a natural phenomenon, leaving aside the more radical aspects of the opposition between nature and convention, the conventional character of silver or gold coinage has to be emphasized. One of the best examples of this tendency is to consider as a move away from nature the change from gold and silver currency to paper (the convertibility of which was backed by state institutions) and later to bank-notes with no guaranteed convertibility, ending up with conventional notes not convertible into gold and having a fixed exchange rate (after the First World War). This change is often seen as a downward movement drawing further and further away from the happy days of a natural and dependable currency, as if the decision to give a certain value to a metal found underground (gold and silver) was not artificial or fictional. The value judgment passed against this fall into the world of the inauthentic, this distance established in relation with the world of nature, rests on a whole set of moral pronouncements based on the intrinsic value of gold and silver, a kind of ethical code for economic activities that would be worth investigating in itself. It is connected with other displays of fetishism (in either money or goods), which will be touched on later on. The classical analysis of fetishism, bordering at times on denunciation, especially in this field, as made by Marx or Freud, rests on philosophical premises which themselves raise a number of questions, but these are not within the scope of this paper.

If in certain circumstances an additional convention applies to the difference in meaning between the terms money and currency (thereby bringing out the problem of the "spirit of the market"), it is part of a more general set of conventions and interconnections. It is no accident indeed that the currency and monetary symbol frequently served as models in analyzing the workings of the language—or a system of signs in general. Well before Mallarme and Saussure, and probably since Plato there were many instances of this kind of comparison. Valery, for example, made much use of this similarity between capital and linguistics, not to mention capital and mind, capital and logos. It can be argued that this goes further than mere analogy, or at least that it is not one among many. Here we are witnessing the emergence of what could be aptly called "the spirit of the market." Two reasons can explain the development.

Insofar as language is the vehicle for economic transactions, information and stock exchange quotations, insofar as the market is fully dependent on communication media—which themselves are constantly evolving on the technical level and whose accelerating pace of change is due to the influence of language on the process of speeding up, then it can be said that the fundamental role played by language in monetary geopolitics ushers in all the implications contained in language: rhetoric, connotations, play-acting, fiction, one could almost add literature, in short all the influences likely to affect the workings of a machinery highly quantifiable and susceptible of clockwork accounting. These influences come in various categories, to do with quality, emotions, imagination, they belong to the realm of fantasies, ideologies, they are fed by irrational swings in public opinion set in motion by rumors and moods. I refer to the microphenomena which govern our present-day geopolitics, such as the mysterious origins of a feeling or a passion, of a sense of anxiety or optimism, not easy to trace either in individuals or communities. The effects of these fleeting mental dispositions can be observed, but never fully analyzed. They are capable of maximum speed, thanks to satellites and information technology, they juggle with time zones all round the globe, and can start historical landslides liable to affect people for long periods, decide of war and peace, work prospects and poverty, condition the way humanity will live right up to villages apparently furthest from the Stock Exchanges of Wall St., London, Paris and Tokyo. Like economic speculation in general, the stage for stock exchange quotations is one of accounting, information, communication and technology, but it is also a language and vocabulary which can never be fully formalized. We are dealing with a "human" phenomenon not to be reduced in mere numbers.

There undoubtedly is a spirit of the market in the sense that the latter is language and cannot be reduced to figures or put into categories. This spirit does not bring economics into disrepute as a science, but it sets a limit to its ambitions, to its autonomy and specificity, it denies it total control through numbers.

These remarks concerned the spirit of the market as language, but now I would like to suggest another one concerning money and language. The distinction made between money and currency is universal by and large, but is not expressed in the same way in all languages. The German sequence or the English one cannot be translated automatically into French without painstaking considerations as the idiom has only one word to apply to the metal found in nature, money as currency or monetary symbol and money as investment endowed, because of its relation with the natural ore, with all kinds of values stemming from the complex and determining action of desire and hatred, appetite and disgust, anal thrift leading to retention, or the rejection of waste, etc. What we call "argent" in French (which is not merely monetary symbol nor the change paid following a purchase, nor the metal to be found in mines or jewelry) cannot be translated by a single word in English or German as silver or *Silber*, nor even strictly speaking *Geld* or money.

Only in the French language does the word "argent" coincide exactly, at least in people's imagination, with both money as means of exchange and the fine shining metal of which coins and jewels are made. Having a bank-note, a bank account, private property, is the same as having money. This is not the case in English or German, and French idioms such as "le temps, c'est de l'argent," "l'argent ne fait pas le bonheur," "prendre pour argent comptant" are not easy to translate. In a way, the spirit of the market also pervades the area of irrational investment, which to say the least offers difficulties to the analyst because it is impossible to evaluate. This kind of investment is multiplied in the course of time, it acquires weight and brings in capital gains through its stratified history. Such a history comes in layers, which affect the investment, not only through the value ascribed to a metal, but also in the semantics of the word or the gap between the practical value and the exchange value of the word. The topic can only be hinted at here: the operation is carried out within the strict limitations imposed by the individual language. Yet the words are supposed to apply to the most universal object, one that knows no cultural barriers, therefore easy to translate. Money is seen as neutral, impersonal, the general equivalent of any exchange or transaction, a substitute universally accepted and shared the world over (although unevenly distributed). The same universal character is supposed to apply when money is regarded as the axis round which gravitate contradictory or ambiguous impulses (yearning for a noble thing or rejection of a vile one which on the one hand can be appropriated and can become synonymous with everything to be possessed, but can also be identified with something to be given up, presented out of sheer generosity or for any other reason.) Above all, the fact that money belongs to the limitless world of language and the written word—the inscription—means that it cannot be contained in monetary accounting or objective economics. Money drives the enterprise in the direction of the infinite or towards regions unknown to accountants, to the edge of an abyss of speculation which lies outside the field of the Stock Exchange or the limits of institutions regulating economic transactions.

We are faced with the distinction first suggested by Aristotle, a distinction pregnant with many ideas even though it might look farfetched for the reasons mentioned above. It emphasizes the difference between "chrematistics" and "economics."

Economics apply to the management of goods pertaining to the "oikos," household, family, community, even the city (nation or state), to the technique necessary to acquire or exchange these goods in relation to needs which are on principle well-determined. Chrematistics on the contrary is boundless, applying to the art of acquiring goods or riches for their own sake, through commerce or speculation, according to the laws of the market, with not limits set and starting from false premises. Aristotle calls it the artificial, distorting element of the chrematistic impulse. It is as if true riches consisted in a large amount of money and this belief lies at the heart of what, from the eighteenth century onwards, came to be called by analogy "money fetishism."

In this sense, if one tried to contrast chrematistics with economics, on the assumption that it is an art or a science, it would appear to be at the core of the market mentality, coinciding with what the market offers beyond any reasonable limit set by our natural needs, beyond a well regulated balance between production and consumption, between the requirements of the home and those of fellow citizens, etc. I strongly suspect that the boundary separating need and desire, or even the opposition between them, just as the one separating the economic or purely monetary market and the spirit of the market becomes blurred from the very first attempt at an exchange. As far as money or currency are concerned, as soon as there is an element of monetary symbol, transfer and a repetition of the operation, the boundary between economics and chrematistics no longer exists, the same being valid for all connected terms of opposition.

This phenomenon of blurred boundaries being self-evident and intrinsic has far-reaching consequences, precisely because their effect cannot be calculated, especially in the area where money is concerned. This is probably at the root of all speculation, meaning financial return on capital which accrues without any work, the fetishistic accumulation of goods and currency, but it also makes it possible to go beyond mere need, as also does the action of desire presumably. It also allows freedom from the imperatives of the balance-sheet, similarly to the act of giving if it exists at all.

At the beginning of the paper we laid the principle: time is of the essence, but now I find that time is short and I must come to conclusions. Let us consider the time limits set for this talk. Round this subject, I shall just mention a few points in passing. Behind the expression "time is money" quoted earlier, equally valid in English and French, there may be more than meets the eye. It may mean that time is a measure for work and production, that is to say it enters into the process of creation and acquisition of riches, which are themselves in theory accountable and can be turned into money, in economic or literary terms. This also means that in the usual sense of the phrase lies the implication that work, being an element of production, plays a vital part in linking time and money. Work would be the connection between time and money, the corner-stone of the statement "time is money" because it represents working hours, even if it applies to capital (we all know that Marx was not the only one among economists to give precedence to a reflection on time and the relation between time, work, production and money). Such might be the common interpretation, justifiably given to the current saying. A saying can be compared to a kind of currency, both valuable and worthless, permanent and devalued, a relic from a common heritage, just like language itself. Nothing is more common than a proverb, like money itself, but equally nothing is less so.

Giving another interpretation to the saying, it could be asserted that money is the equivalent of time. In this case, not because time allows to gain money, as was said, either in the form of working hours, or because money itself is made to fructify, but because money saves time. As a substitute for anything, it saves time during the process of exchanging goods and property; it speeds up transactions no end, not only through making it possible to find substitutes, but by putting and end to the principle of barter. In ushering in the reign of repetition, substitution, that is to say neutralizing the individual characteristics of the objects concerned in the exchange, it allows to quantify them and give them a mathematical value, which in the first place means a blatant neutralization of time. This is the reason why, by the way, the saving of time achieved by the new communication technology in the operations of the stock Exchange, together with speculative movements, cannot have occurred by chance. It validates the equation between money and time, showing an acceleration of the pace of society, acting as a means of measuring and managing time. Money is time gained, time saved (I started my talk with a mention of the need to save time) or a void in time, a pause helping to save time. Between the spirit of the market and modern techniques there is no cleavage, they follow the same rules. The economics of time as measure means that time is endowed with a spatial dimension. In this respect money is, not only as currency, but as spirit of the market, as the force behind the chrematistic desire which projects itself beyond the economic world—in the narrow sense in which Aristotle understood it—a time economy, a clock in which technology, especially information technology, if it can be distinguished from technology in a general sense, does not merely play the part of an instrument, but carries it along with its own momentum.

These few observations bring to light at least two problems (those of ethics on the one hand and signature on the other which are intimately bound) that I can only sketch in their outline. They both have to do with the fundamental concepts of substitution, repetition and neutralization mentioned earlier. These three words have in common an element of indifference. Money is indifferent because its symbols must be equal and similar (there is no difference between two ten francs coins or two fifty francs notes; basic indifference due to the rules of convention, arbitrary choice of symbols leading to repetition, possibility of transfer from one place to another all over the world). The same applies to the source or the bearer of money which, as the saying goes, has no odor. These three examples of indifference (substitution, repetition and neutralization) cannot be separated and are an essential component of the concept of money: as quantifiable value, as monetary symbol or as an expression of what is desirable, infinitely desirable, whether in a simple or ambivalent form.

Let us now examine ethics and signature. Ethics taken in the broad sense belong to the moral, legalistic and political spheres. Being unconcerned with specific cases, the experience of finance can be seen as an introduction to operations of substitution, repetition and neutralization. Due to this lack of concern, together with connotations of non-value, (money representing waste, excrement, an object of fetishist desire, a vehicle for greed and anal retention—but "odorless"), for moral, legalistic or political considerations, human reason should free itself from the grip of money: not only from that of economics, monetary accounting, but above all from the spirit of the market. Often giving rise to a feeling of shame, according to Freud, money belongs to a category of things which can replace one another: excrement, child, penis, weapon, gift. Among these, it seems to indicate an equivalence and following this a possibility of substitution within the series due to basic indifferentiation. Freud early on insisted on the part played by payment in psychiatric treatment and emphasized the fact that civilized people consider money as a sexual object, with a great deal of hypocrisy and inconsistency.

Yet the attitude of despising money is not without contradictions. These are expressed in ideological declarations and superior airs taken by some: the landowner prides himself in being above the tradesman, the speculator, the usurer, often represented as a Levantine or a Jew by Western Christian artists. These dividing lines go through the community of philosophers; there are some who concern themselves with financial matters and some who claim to be uninterested. Among the lofty statements contrasting morality and the market principle, let us recall Kant's distinguishing between two notions which are closely related yet separate, dignity and price, *Wurde* and *Preis*. Dignity is invested with unconditional value which should be respected as an absolute because of the moral law from which it springs. It is not subject to negotiation and stands above the market. Unlike dignity whose value cannot be measured, price is conditional, hypothetical, negotiable and expressed in figures.

"In the realm of ends," Kant wrote, "everything has a price or dignity. What has a price can be replaced at will by something else, as an equivalent; inversely what stands higher than any price whatsoever, what cannot be found an equivalent ever, is endowed with dignity." In other words, as it stands higher than price, dignity belongs to a category which we qualify as "priceless." Your neighbor, being infinitely precious, in his dignity, is priceless. Vice-versa, everything in a person (in myself taken as an individual) that is valuable and respectable in the absolute sense, that is non negotiable, bears the stamp of dignity as an end in itself. But what is such, in someone's ego or in mine? This unaccountable characteristic remains hard to define. Could it be an ego? is it the most secret or the most universal element? What happens to individual features? Shall we call what is above the market price a reasonable being? or on the contrary, is the subject liable, as a working unit, to turn into merchandise?

Kant continued:

> What touches on human inclinations and general needs has a commercial value [*marktpreis*]; what corresponds to a particular taste, without answering a need, that is to say satisfies our yearning to exercise our mental capacities, can be said to have an emotional price [*Affectionpreis*]; but the condition that makes it possible to say that something is an end in itself [*Zweck an sich selbst*], has not only a relative value, that is to say a price, but an internal value, that is to say dignity [*Wurde*].

The horrendous problem raised by this basic distinction was hinted at when we touched on the question of being and it lies in the fact that if dignity is threatened by the price estimated, by the market or by money, (for example human dignity, that of a reasonable being, but also of any end in itself—human right being the best of all in Kant's opinion), equally as principle of equivalence and substitution it represents the necessary element of equality among specific entities, therefore it makes it morally impossible, unthinkable even, to choose between two absolutes, two entities. Two men, for example, share an equal amount of moral, legal and political dignity, whatever their differences in any sphere (social, economic, biological, sexual, psychological or intellectual, etc.). A choice has to be made between these two equivalent data which neutralize each other, two heterogeneous entities which do not differ in value, but it is perilous: it is exposed to constant threat and most often impossible to carry out or only a contrariety.

At this point we must negotiate what is not negotiable. This imperative is not an easy option taken from empirical considerations, the very difficulty to reach a decisions imposes it on us. A new dimension is added and with it moral, legal as well as political responsibility. This happens before any negotiation between imperative and hypothetical, between the unconditional and the conditional, the non-negotiable and the negotiable. Indeed it is the existence of money, of a price, that is to say the principle of equivalent, which allows also to neutralize the differences and reach the individual core on which dignity and universal right are based. The realization of another person's dignity implies consciousness of his or her unique difference, of course, but it only becomes possible through a measure of indifference, through the neutralization of social, economic, ethnic, sexual, etc. differences. Going beyond the field of knowledge and any objective criteria and any objective criteria, this neutralization alone ushers in the realm of dignity, that is to say to the fact that each and everyone is worth as much as the next man or woman, in the sense that he or she is beyond value, that is to say priceless. The rejection of money or of its principle of abstract indifference, the scorn cast on calculations go hand in hand with the destruction of morality, of law—for example in the case of electoral democracy which is only concerned with "votes," etc.

It is always useful to consider opposites, and as much care and devotion should be given to the analysis of the contrary aspects of money and the fetishistic appeal of goods.

The other problem we mentioned, that of signature, touches on a time of absolute specificity. It coincides with the fast disappearance not of money, but of the monetary symbol in its so called material form; let us insist on the "so-called material form." Further analysis would show the highly problematic contents of the word "matter"; above all when they say, and I occasionally used this ambiguous expression, that money is increasingly dematerialized (credit card, electronic exchanges, etc.), the problem of absolute specificity goes hand in hand with the experience of signing one's name. Through the history of monetary symbols, "money" (coins made of gold or silver, bank-notes not convertible into gold and silver, as often happened after the first world war—or whose convertibility is backed by the state, or even at a fixed rate) in principle belongs to the bearer of the anonymous monetary symbol. The emergence of the letter of exchange and cheque appealed mainly to the person who was to sign his name, him or herself, immediately, here and now. Even if the signature can be delegated or imitated, there remains the fundamental validity of the name bearer's commitment to cover payment, recognition of debt, etc. The de-materialization of money, without restoring anonymity to the bearer, became embodied in the system of metal currency and bank-notes and imposed a numerical signature, without a personal hand-written name; this kind of signature replaced both the non-numerical one and the monetary symbol, its paper or metal expression. What is called de-materialization does not mean the disappearance or spiritualization of matter (still it could be argued that there occurred an idealization of money based on a "material" support), but is only the exchange of one support for another, from something visible as stuff that the bearer holds in his hand or his pocket (metal or paper) to an electronic support which enters data extraneous to the person. Though the authority of a name, a personal commitment is involved at a certain stage, and remains a condition of the electronic money system (at one remove, since someone must sign with his "own" hand on receipt of the secret code number), these phenomenal differences, these changes in the physical expression of commercial exchanges are bound to have enormous repercussions on individual subjects and societies as regards living experience, body awareness, relations with one's clothes, hand, with what is given and received in general. Indeed the consciousness of one's name is bound to be affected since it can be replaced by a secret number.

As I have already taken too much of the audience's time and because I make it a principle not to mention a book I have recently published on a related subject, I propose to conclude with an anecdote which took place recently in a Paris station. On my way back from the North I had to use the telephone. Seeing a young English couple embarrassed because they did not have a telephone card, I dialed the number they wanted using my own card and left it with them. They made as if to pay for it and I waved them off. Did I give something, how much? I firmly believe that the question is best left unanswered, and shall explain the reason why if there is time for a discussion.

Money and Hyper-Money

Marc Guillaume

Money is a double sided concept which is the reason why it belongs to worlds which stand apart. The word is highly ambiguous due to a gap between its meaning and its position in our mental imagery.

On the one hand it is a household word, endowed with slang equivalents and colloquial expressions. Children become familiar with it at an early stage, together with its counterpart in the real world: money you are given, or you find, that can be stolen, counted out as pocket-money—these are various experiences of great significance for the future. But, on the other hand, any real understanding of the word demands that it be set in the social and economic environment to which it belongs: currency, the economic field and in the last resort, the economic sphere.

The following definitions will be taken as a basis:

- silver: material support for coinage;
- money: medium used for accounting, making reserve funds, operating transactions in the economic field;
- economic field: the whole spectrum of operations needed for production, consumption and exchanges of goods or services;
- economic sphere: practices and mental representations arising from economic value.

The former definitions are familiar, but the notion of an economic sphere which underlies the economic field though not often mentioned deserves attention. We are dealing with a set of practices (as seen in the work place, the consumer society...), together with social relations arising from these practices, intellectual representations and theories (in which knowledge and beliefs are combined). In short it amounts to a philosophy, a world view, which corresponds to that of the industrial nations, scene of the global economy. I shall concentrate on one aspect of this philosophy, one that throws some light on the tendency present in the global economy to distort the most solidly established values, meaning the acceptance or even glorification of permanent warfare as a natural or even desirable state of affairs. Of course, we are talking about economic war, which quite openly are waged by nations through commercial enterprises.

It is a war full of perils and tragedies for the third world countries, not to mention disturbing consequences for the more advanced ones.

Though economists devote much time to money and the economic field, they are not usually concerned with the economic sphere. They would have to turn into sociologists or anthropologists to do so and would be afraid of losing prestige. Conversely, sociologists by and large, have little time for the economic sphere. The barriers that separate university departments mean that a blind spot exists as to the foundations of our culture (in the sense of anthropologists). In spite of the vast amount of knowledge and of the claim made by modern intellectuals to a rational explanation of the world, our societies, like former ones, are unable to account fully for the root of their cohesion and for the changes that might occur.

Economists are even less interested in money. First of all, because its status is dependent on the economic sphere which works out the common approach to it, next, because entirely different disciplines would be called for in order to gain real understanding. Even specialists in currency hardly ever mention the word money, apart from a few historians of coinage. The latter are not really economists and have to fight an exhausting battle against the erroneous ideas advanced by witless economists (cf. J.M. Servet's paper). In conclusion money is a subject of little interest to economists. Other researchers are more concerned and there are countless books on the social impact of money as distinct from the strictly economic aspect (still to be observed in modern society, as for example the burning of bank-notes which is part of funereal rites in China). Besides, since the first findings of Freud (*Character and anal Eroticism*, 1908), followed by those of Ferenczi (*On the Sources of the Interest in Money*, 1914), psychoanalysis has ceaselessly explored the role of money the various pathologies of daily life (cf. A. de Mijolla's paper; also the recent book of S. Viderman, *De l'argent en psychanalyse et au-dela*, PUF, 1992).

This is all very well but it throws light on the basic division that was mentioned earlier as regards disciplines. On the one hand, we have currency, an agent (for reserve funds, transactions and accounting) which is dependent on prices themselves dependent on exchange values. It is a neutral agent, with no affective connotation, a mere technical instrument. On the other hand, we have money (argent) which is anything but sterile or neutral. It is a breeding ground for many passions, pathologies or fantasies: being the universal equivalent for all possible goods, the basis of all desires, it is bound to leave its mark deep down on the human psyche, including, obviously, the subconscious; deep down also at the heart of any society.

This is division of labor at its highest: economists deal with money as a neutral agent and analyze its utilitarian aspects. Anthropologists, historians and psychoanalysts ponder the vital questions, but in another setting (in societies distant in time or geographical space) or from the point of view of individual disturbances without confronting these vital questions with the economic sphere to which we belong.

This partitioning, exacerbated as it is by a growing specialization in modern knowledge, could not prevent some transversal forays intended to cast some light on the working of society as a whole, or to explore some individual cases. These occurrences are few and the link between money and currency has been largely ignored, or at least neglected. Those who tried acting as bridges between distant territories were labeled specialists in one discipline but not in the other. They preached in the wilderness and failed to acquire followers.

There are nevertheless extreme or exceptional situations in which the notions of currency and money are spectacularly bound together. The resulting analysis is a condemnation of an unhealthy appetite for money. These situations apply either to speculation, illicit trafficking, prostitution or gambling which evoke derogatory terms such as easy money or laundering of dirty money....

This partitioning between money and currency while usually respected by researchers and in real life becomes blurred in common parlance. No doubt in most languages there is a distinction between two aspects of the notion of money, one of which concerns the economic field. The couple "argent/monnaie" corresponds in a slightly milder way to "money/currency" and "Geld/Munze" as well as the Japanese "okane/kahei," etc. However, in practice this distinction is not always respected. In French the term "argent" is the normal way to refer to phenomena relating to capital gain or changes in the economic sphere. This is the meaning of such expressions as "drug money" (applying to movements of capital which amount to 120 billion dollars world-wide), golden boys replacing the old type City gents particularly in London, and the "money society" indicating the ugly face of capitalism. The same extensive use of the term can be found in German, which does not make the task of translation any easier. When Marx wrote: "money, womb of all perversions, destroyer of all social relations," he referred to the currency used by the emerging capitalist order rather to money in general which plays a part in every form of social relations.

In this wide sense it can be equated to a figure of speech, as one talks of the sword of justice, meaning the law, and money can represent, according to circumstances, currency or certain economic ills, the Marxist notion of value, etc. This interpretation is obviously valid, but does not give the full story. If it were only a figure of speech it would have fallen into disuse, as happens so often to other expressions in every language. Behind the rhetoric lie a host of meanings hidden in a confusion which can teach us much. Money as hotbed of passions and myths is not only a vivid way of describing the economic sphere, it is a vital component of the latter which cannot be dispensed with, though it does not come under scrutiny. In general terms, the kind of civilization superimposed by the economic power on various societies is characterized by a dual aspect: on the one hand utilitarian values are produced together with a ruthless search for efficiency and rationalization, but on the other hand it feeds on myths and provides a lay religion, as Rousseau pointed out. The economic sphere remains a religious one, a kind of social bond woven out of shared beliefs and myths: the myth of a necessary economic struggle, of growth and happiness reached through an accumulation of material goods, the myth of the defeat of illness and death through technical advances, etc.

Money, under its various meanings, sums up this basic illusion, the dual aspect of the economic order. It combines two faces, as it lies at the heart of the utilitarian philosophy, as it is handled with increasing efficiency by specialized institutions, but remains meanwhile the rock on which a universal longing for happiness rests (money does not bring happiness according to the proverb, as if refusing the temptation to admit the opposite), and a condition for the process of deification and desacralization needed for acceptance of the economic order.

It is impossible here to analyze in detail the ambiguous status of money. Yet a short introduction was called for to deal with a well-delineated subject, that of the new monetary techniques as seen against a background of hypotheses in order to avoid reducing them to mere technical progress. The changes affecting money as an artificial creation will be examined, bearing in mind the two-pronged relation between money and the economic order, not forgetting the underlying violence in both of them. The guiding principle of this enquiry will be such: the new monetary techniques (NMT), in appearance try to conceal, even to eliminate money as the origin of passions, capable of inflaming man's imagination. This attempt at "purifying" money and making it sterile is, however, doomed to fail at least partially, and we have to investigate the semiological innovations which accompany technical advances. It is not enough here to point out the dematerialization of money. Through an examination of the NMT's emerging uses—mainly those that are independent of economic agents—a new pattern of economic practices and representations can be established.

FIELDS OF APPLICATION OF THE NEW MONETARY TECHNIQUES

City life—in France the ancestor of NMT in public transport was the orange pass card which was later copied in provincial towns, using modern electronic devices. One such has been introduced in Lyon (a card like a telephone card with no name on it). It allows for payment at each stage of the journey, with the card activated on sight on entering and leaving the bus. The fare is automatically calculated and debited. The amount paid and credit left can be checked on the liquid crystal screen of the card. It sounds rather far-fetched and even suspicious, but it makes possible other innovations: at Blois, for instance, an electronic card is valid on buses for which payment varies according to the time of day. The saying "Time is money" acquires a new dimension.

If we look beyond public transport, we find that local councils in very small communities were the first to experiment with electronic money in the department of Ariege in 1986. Cards with memory were used for school canteens, crèches and school buses. This early technological experiment was imitated in larger places, while other councils introduced multi-services cards (bus, taxi, boat at La Rochelle). Another ambitious project was launched at the Metz Technopolis with university restaurants combining with accommodation services and telecommunications.

This urban system of electronic money offers many advantages: efficiency and convenience for users, the progressive image it gives to a city (the card can be used for publicity and information), less unpaid bills for the administration and possibility of flexible fares).

As a rule, it makes charges for local council services less troublesome. Hence they are given an aura and become more attractive than consumers goods in general.

These first experiments do not go without certain difficulties: users distrust, cash-flow problems for humble householders, technical hiccups of various kinds and above all difficulties in combining private and public accounting.

In the short term other fields of application will emerge (motorway tolls, parking fees calculated according to specific qualifications, etc.) which will impose some kind of regulation on this new monetary development.

MASS SERVICES:

The first sector to introduce new forms of payment was the Telephone service. Electronic cards put an end to vandalism and ensured that payment was made in two separate operations (you buy a card first to be debited later). With the approaching change to a personal telephone number (not dependent on the place of residence) many technical advances will be made possible by this card in the near future (it could even be replaced by a code number, telephone bills payment would be completely dematerialized, as is already the case with mobile and home telephones.) The same phenomenon is happening in the world of telecommunications through a clever device in use for public telephones adjusting the charge to the length and nature of the service provided. This is one reason why the operation has been a success in France, while it was not so in other European countries.

As regards television the situation is the opposite, the pay as you view system never having taken off, but being widespread in Canada and the United States. This form of payment is unpopular because it goes against the grain not having free access to TV viewing in exchange for a symbolic fee.

On the whole, the aim of electronic money is to make payment of telecommunications as discrete as possible. It also allows for flexibility (time and length of viewing) taking into account the quality of services.

Alongside with communications, the same phenomenon occurred in the area of leisure and can be observed in some theme parks or sports centers to be found in increasing numbers in developed countries. It should be pointed out that this way of paying for a service is not a novelty, having long been practiced in the world of gambling (prizes in kind, tokens, etc.) and is common nowadays in casinos or sites of the holiday business of Club Mediterranee where it forms no small part of its success.

The health sector offers great scope for this kind of payment. Expenses are largely covered by a complex system established on the edge of the fiscal system and the introduction of a personal card would be a bonus there. The advantages of such a scheme would also be to make direct payment (not taxable) less obvious and better suited to individual situations. Such a card could offer other services apart from the monetary aspect (data bank for each individual) but is taking a long time to put in place.

It could easily happen in the meanwhile that the money circulating in local services would be "carried" by a few specific cards (transport, communications, health, training, etc.) as an equivalent to credit cards in private consumption.

CONSUMPTION:

In retail outlets bank-notes have lost ground to checks which are themselves being replaced by credit cards (there are 500 million of them in use throughout the world). Paying with a card improves the quality of goods and services. This in-built invoicing has been so successful that one must assume that it is here to stay. As a rule the convenience of this type of payment which makes it hardly noticeable ensures that it has an effect on the volume of sale and on consumers' patterns of behavior.

Besides representing an added attraction for the goods or services made available, the card imparts a certain amount of prestige to the owner. Like an identity card or a visiting card, it acts as support to a code number which allows a computerized handling of figures, although the slogan they put forward is "a member not a number." Moreover, a hierarchy can be observed among cards which cannot be used universally for commercial exchanges. Thus these new monetary forms reflect certain aspects of the old types of currency which could only be issued by qualified people and were available to a select few, according to the kind of goods involved. Credit cards therefore combine technical efficiency with long-forgotten outmoded features ensuring an adequate return on the use of money—which French banks have been unable to do in the matter of charges for check-books—in the form of a yearly charge and differed payment plus commissions imposed on shopkeepers.

BANKS:

Modern payment techniques and transfers have proved beneficial since they mean a smaller number of checks and more rational organization. They represent also a platform for the offer of other services. In reality, the customer is charged for some of the operations that used to be carried out by banks as a matter of course (automatic cash dispensers, computerized transfers). The customer is both held at arm's length (which suits him fine since no one enjoys being confronted by an angry bank-manager) and tightly enclosed by the new techniques. "The influence of computers in banking greatly widens the centuries-old role of these institutions which now enter people's homes (long-distance settling of bills) and know no limit in space (world-wide foreign exchange), encompass both the present (cash) and the future (credit, insurance, retirement pensions) until their services pervade all aspects of daily life."

The new techniques do not belong exclusively to the world of banking, other bodies can set themselves up as competitors at any time through them. Faced with this kind of pressure the problem of financing costs gets steadily more acute, being both technical (how to adjust charges realistically) and one of social justice (how to avoid levying a high charge on the needy clients). Nowadays in France a minority pays for the benefits realized by banks, while the majority gets Scot free. It is impossible to imitate the insurance companies (premiums at adjustable rates according to the risks taken), charging for check-books would be highly unpopular and the brutal step of closing accounts which do not pay for themselves can only be taken occasionally. The NMT will probably provide a way out of these imbalances in the long term but there will remain the problem of the poorest section of the community not having access to these modern ways of payment.

A FEW GUIDELINES: ARE WE HEADED FOR A HYPER-CURRENCY?

Talking about new monetary forms, one always mentions dematerialization first. It is a phenomenon easy to observe which seems irresistible. It is striking to see the overwhelming change from coins to bank-notes and more recently to more elusive supports. Yet more significant changes are occurring below the surface. Under the phenomenon of dematerialization there is a central authority registering money transfers. When money takes the form of cash, its circulation may be more difficult at times, but its movement is not obvious, or at least it can remain secret. With dematerialization money leaves an imprint, through the work of computers it can be traced at all times (or almost and increasingly so). This monetary memory has practical effects on the control that nations exert in the matter of taxes, directly or through measures of self-discipline, over the exchanges of the market economy. Money is no longer likely, as in the past, to be involved in illegal trafficking.

The phenomenon of dematerialization increases the fluidity and the speed of movements. This trend is most in evidence and far-reaching in respect to financial institutions which now transfer their cash according to exchange rates fluctuations. The consequences have been observed and analyzed by many researchers already. Here again the reign of the computer introduced new rhythms in the circulation of money.

If widespread use of computers has brought about control and speed (as regards financial operators) it has also provided less obvious means of action for consumers. Resources can be allocated as soon as they become available, thereby delays are reduced and even the possibility of a change or mind which can affect freedom of choice eventually. Modern facilities encourage private consumption on borrowed money, especially for young people. They facilitate payment for collective activities, transport, communications, taxes, as we saw earlier, they give access to a new range of customers in the area of diversified saving units that may be self-managed. Thus they are capable of mopping up all available funds thanks to computer-based mechanisms and easier transfers. Thus a whole range of jobs are brought into play to deal with the funds available to every citizen. In the same way as data and documents are handled (thanks to telecommunications and hypertexts) with the required information brought home to users (in the opposite direction of what happened in the past), computer-based movement of money brings the possibility of spending and modulated saving to any person who enjoys real or anticipated purchasing power. In this sense one can talk of hyper-money.

The result of this accelerated transfer of resources is to leave individuals with nothing but pocket-money, this being true also of high-income couples. Marx fully realized that the proletarian's money is not, in spite of sharing the same system of accounting, identical in character with the capitalist's. The former is frivolous, the other fruitful, since its size makes for the acquisition of a work force which produces capital gain. Hyper-money creates a web round individuals and reduces direct investments which involves a risk; it helps to sterilize ordinary resources and thus separates even more sharply the two kinds of money.

The new monetary forms are part of a process of sterilization of violence in the world of finance. The generalization of commercial exchanges makes relations between people more objective (or less subjective). This is one aspect of what Marx called the fetishism of money. The fact that everything capable of being subjected to a commercial exchange (product for consumption, services, work force, etc.) acquires a higher value, quite apart from the relations between buyer and seller and their link with the object exchanged, makes for a violent reduction of the whole range of the social relations involved in exchanges. We all know that this process of reduction has met over the centuries in Europe with sharp cultural and religious resistance; for example Catholics preached the doctrine of a "fair price," charging interest on loans was forbidden as well as entering into insurance schemes (as late as 1788 in France), etc. Even today, capitalist societies of similar level of development have different levels of monetarization and emotional reaction to it. There are indeed wide differences regarding trade in human organs or genetic engineering.

This violent character of money is in reality an intrinsic feature of the economic order, the organization of markets (which is only a form of economic gain, but in reality an overwhelming one) and the use made of money being the tools which bring it to fruition. This abstract violence has become part of our everyday life and remains present in currency as it obeys its laws on a daily basis.

Besides the abstract type of violence which accompanies the phenomenon of reification, there is a more blatant form of seizing everyone who sees the realization of his wishes draw near. There is no need to explain further the attraction exerted: we are gripped by greed, money not currency becoming our master.

In a commercial exchange, both elements of money and currency put us under pressure. We all experienced the banality induced by commercialization: a unique piece of collection goes to an unenlightened amateur who happens to be rich, conversation (by telephone) has a price, etc. There is a sad feeling attached to parting with money, as it is the key to the achievement of so many other desires, mixed with pleasure at obtaining a particular object (which "satisfies" a desire, but for how long?) and uneasiness about the fairness of the transaction. Commerce is thus shot through with violence, but also exorcises it by means of regulations, ritual and because the exchange seems to answer the necessary balance, money acquires a human dimension. Montesquieu was one to point out the benefits of fair trading in human relations.

It so happens that NMT help to widen the field of valorization (through them it is easy to pay for communications going via the media, for space when it is saturated and the risks incurred by others, etc.) while, at the same time, they conceal the monetary operation. Any element of cruelty, of giddiness that money might have presented, is eliminated. For some time it has become awkward to pay large amounts of money in cash (not only due to tax control regulations making it illegal). The modern trend appears to contain a paradox: as money pervades everything, its material support is fast disappearing.

Stretching from commercial transactions deprived of material basis to automatic charging for expenditure which goes almost unnoticed, even the world of gambling being controlled and sterilized (small losses and gains liable to be taxed—though there are exceptions and various centers of population still handle large sums of money) this all-embracing presence-absence of money is part of a wider development. After seeing societies doomed to normalization we are entering the era of self-regulation. Everything that might appear as breaking the law, cruelty, loss of control—at the same time acting as exorcism—becomes forbidden, frowned at and swept under the carpet. When Serge Gainsbourg burnt a 500 F bank-note live on TV he met with universal disapproval, though the gesture benefited the viewers rather than hurting them, since it helped deflation.

In this neutral world what happens to human passions, to the burning feeling that money used to arouse? Do we still dream of running our hands through a mountain of gold coins? We have now nothing to compare with Balzac's imaginings or the place money held in F. Scott Fitzgerald's novels, or with Mallarme's reference to "les monnaies a demi effacees qu'on se passe en silence" as a symbol of meaningless phrases expressing the joy of being alive and meeting fellow human beings. Money has lost its role as social cement or fuel of dissension, it has collapsed on itself as modern techniques allowed it to master every situation.

THE LETTER AND METAL

Pierre Chaunu

An item in the initial stages of television advertising proclaimed: "you always need peas in the home." This was at the end of the "swinging thirties" that the much lamented Jean Fourastié so admired. I would suggest a different version better suited to the austerity of this sad decade: even at such a serious conference as that of the Monde at Le Mans, before we get down to business, we often resort to "rent a historian." God save us!

Well before the looming 500th anniversary which follows on the tail of our French bicentenary, and will take place in the city of Seville, in association with Genoa and Antwerp, I was already what is usually called an economic historian. Prior to the "good old computer" and using a Bic biro, a stone-age Olivetti, and with the help of my wife, I had even counted a lot of ships, many doubloons and several bundles of merchandise. But that was a long time ago and later I was drawn to other things. Consequently I shall beg you not to expect too much erudition, but at best a disenchanted look from the distance of Sirius.

Initially I was asked to deal with the sixteenth century. Shrewdly you finally allowed me a vast field extending from Rome to the Enlightenment, which is a wise precaution in view of my bad habit of rambling and darting about.

What about money between these two periods, with a backdrop that stretches over a thousand years? In the area where money existed…, this excluding over those thousand years, much of the time, not only a lot of people, but more than half the population of the planet. If we were to use a map of the 76 ethno-anthropological areas, established by Fernand Braudel, with myself hot on his tail, from G.H. Hewes' work, *Cultures et peuples primitifs vers 1500* (*Cultures and Primitive Peoples Around 1500*) and using a methodology that might need an overhaul) prior to the terrific opening up at the start of the sixteenth century, this would show that 8/10ths of the earth's surface did not use on a regular basis any form of money. These were, in diachronic terms, pre-neolithic populations, of which there were still many. Some subsistence farmers who were semi-nomadic and do not have much use for money. Yet this 8/10ths area of the world did not account for more than a quarter of mankind.

The Amerindian communities living in the uplands(amounting to 90% of the inhabitants of the still unnamed Americas) in the same way that literacy was in its early stages among them, did not master the use of currency. Money would only enter America through transfer and accumulation only after the European invasion. It influenced pre-monetary and crude monetary systems, clearly much less advanced, of China and India even prior to the discrete cultural influence of the foreign presence in coastal waters. This is illustrated by the decline of the *ratio* with gold becoming more important in China than silver. About 62-63 billion people existed prior to 1600 and 64 billion prior to 1700; out of the total of 64 billion lives we can estimate that approximately 10 billion (10 to 12) encountered at least once something resembling a little, or in some way related to what we call money. Please forgive such a silly remark. If I can stretch the point a bit further, out of the 85 billion people who have existed up until now, 35 billion have come into contact with, known and used in their daily lives a wide range of currencies (in the form of metal, paper, printed matter or the electronic variety). Something like a third therefore, considering the recent increase in the world's population. Yet 50 billion at least has never experienced it.

What is the use of history? Possibly to put things into perspective. Applying this idea to Fernand Braudel's work, which I find fascinating, I suggested the notion of a "global weighing" operation. Here is an example.

If you play this little game, which might seem stupid, you will recognize an obvious correlation by using a complementary approach. In order for there to be this monetary phenomenon there has to be a gathering of people. Symbolically we might take one thousand people in a square in Jericho. The first assembly ever of one thousand people, ten thousand years ago, that is to say the neolithic revolution had started somewhere. Yet this condition, even though it is essential, is not sufficient. Money, this perfect tool, like language, for communicating and exchanging is very closely related to the latter—an animal might, at the very most, swap something for something else but would never go on from primitive binary exchange to the complex third party exchange which is a monetary exchange.

Money is not on the same level as a modulated cry, which is a signal, expressing an emotion or a call. Money is of the order of "true language," a sophisticated human language. In a word, the real correlation on a planetary or global scale takes place not at the initial level of an oral language that has a grammar and rules of semantics, but at a further level of developed language endowed with a written form.

Money and writing, writing and money appear roughly concomitantly in terms of the whole history of human phenomena. The global correlation of language/money comes into effect at a late stage after the appearance of writing. No doubt there would not exist a currency without the written word. Probably for a long time there was no written word without the existence of currency.

The sixteenth century, my field, but also because we celebrate the quinquennial anniversary (thankfully following on the heels of the French bicentenary) spurs me on to examine the Americas; these complicated civilizations in the high plateaux with there efficient agricultural systems did not really master writing (developed writing rather than rough script), nor did they have a true currency. This relative backwardness resulted in the search for gold and capture of native gold which accompanied the first wave of "conquistadors."

It was wise of you to give me the sixteenth century to ruminate over. Since contrary to what is said the sixteenth century was at the very end of an age, the only really worthwhile age being that of ideas, and not at the beginning, as has superficially been claimed, following the great period of discovery.

A date to remember, the real turning-point was not 1492 which we celebrate (we never celebrate more than a side-show) but 1609, nine years after the discovery of the glassblowers of Middleborough, which was the day when Galileo turned his telescope—which was then ten years old—skywards.

"From the bottom of the ocean come new stars"—meaning the new technique brought about twice as much information in one century as was possible to gain previously as compared to a ratio of one to two over the preceding two thousand years. thousand years. For in 1611, Galileo could claim, in the only universal language of the day—Latin, that he had the privilege of having seen, in only one year, twenty times as much as all the people together had ever seen over 5,500 years. This Florentine, I will give you this, was slightly exaggerating, he liked to brag, yet only slightly.

In terms of language, of knowledge, which is the most important element, that is to say the mass of information available and its processing, which is the sole motor of history, what matters is tangible evidence and the means to increase it, far more than the caravel. Then space opened up ("the eternal silence of infinite places" and a century later came the crowning explosion, under the glare of the microscope, scrutinizing fossils that are like arabesques embedded in stone, of the realization that man had lived far longer than hitherto believed and the world even more so.

In the main, I can only position myself before the real upheaval of the mass of information available to man and the resulting processing. Metal is there, letters can be inscribed in it, but the main elements of a sophisticated monetary system will fall into place only later following the mathematical classification of "nature" and, *a fortiori,* of society "written in a geometrical language" if I may use the 1620 saying of Galileo and Descartes.

Do I need to recall the main events of this period which has been well documented over the past fifty years and which is so familiar to everyone?

It all started, or rather started again, in Italy during the eleventh century. In terms of exchange techniques the high Middle Ages and the low Classical period appears to provide a backdrop. The letter of exchange that was sent from Athens to Pontus, according to the trustworthy testimony of Isocrates' *Trapezetics*, has disappeared just as the theory of the sun as center of the world and the calculations of Erastosthenes. In any case I am rather reluctant to draw parallels between elements known through ancient sources and the modern world. Recently the fallacy was exposed in the matter of reading and writing levels. It is wise to compare what is truly comparable.

The Latin speaking self-contained West, a world with no empty spaces such as was never seen before, changed all terms of reference. The main axis of communications, after the relative split that occurred following the rapid incursion of Islam from the east to the south and the west, was that still linking the two parts of the Mediterranean. This linked Italy which was partly Byzantine with the Byzantine Empire which had shrunk but was the principal heir to what remained of classical antiquity.

The eleventh century in Italy saw the emergence of the most simple mechanisms of commercial capitalism which would basically led to the annexation of the Americas and penetration of island cultures and isolated civilizations. As well as the time-honoured loan with security and exchange of currencies there is proof that orders were received in Venice, a puny settlement preserved by its situation on a lagoon, as early as 976. There are numerous company contracts still intact from the eleventh century onwards. For big business, there was the maritime loan which involved a high risk and where the onus of insurance rested on a proto-capitalist, the lender. The first *colleganza* contract appeared in Venice in 1072-73 and in Genoa a little later in the twelfth century under the name of *societas maris*. These two mechanisms were instrumental in effecting fundamental changes enabling the creative surge of the twelfth century—which was the crucial period—and the start of the thirteenth century. They meant that logistical support for the crusades could be put in place. The enterprise being an unwieldy affair which bore witness to the new power of the Latin-speaking West and a driving force for greater exertion.

This structure was based on a very limited money supply. This supply was fed by silver and copper from south eastern Germany, Bohemia, Hungary, and Tyrol, and gold from Sudan which was brought over the Sahara on the backs of camels.

Vittorino Magalhaes Godinho has identified the parts of this mechanism and evaluated it. He emphasizes the transition around the thirteenth century from what he calls "Muslim gold to German silver."

What crossed the Sahara can be calculated by the fleets of caravans. Fifty tons per year of gold which was less than what a single caravel could carry and so as to make up the deficit incurred by Black Africa the balance was made up with slaves and about hundred kilos of gold dust. Silver became more important when the needs became acute.

Let us step back a little. There were the well-known maritime routes of the Mediterranean, and after 1291, the straits of Gibraltar commonly used to link the countries bordering on the North Sea and the Mediterranean. Furthermore there were the land-based trade routes for which deals were clinched at fairs in the Champagne region, which provided a fair ground for the letter of exchange devised by Italian merchants who developed a high degree of mastery over it together with a thorough expertise in land and maritime trade. These techniques are well known and their ingenuity augured well for future innovations.

These technical miracles reduced the need for costly and dangerous transport of precious metal and allowed a vast increase in the volume of trade in relation to the money supply, were put at the disposal of two huge consumers, the central administration of the Church that dealt with indulgences and dispensations and above all central governments that made it impossible for princes to manage with their personal income (*ordinaire*), and forced them to raise taxes (exceptional ones that quickly became more and more "normal" and de facto an annual imposition). Thus this became the rule by the end of the thirteenth and the start of the fourteenth centuries with Philippe le Bel, in France, followed by England on a more modest scale (a quarter of the resources of the French King).

Some time ago I managed to calculate the weight in quality silver of taxes year-in year-out, using figures provided by J.J. Clamageran. This amounts to, at the end of the thirteenth century in France which was rich and had a large population, a figure fluctuating from one year to the next between 27.5 and 61.5 tons of quality silver which was available to the royal administration over the whole realm. The fourteenth century stayed at 25-30 tons per year. The ransom of Jean the Good, which was seemed monstrous, was for 163 tons. Charles VII and Louis XII had 55 tons and 47 tons respectively. In the first part of the sixteenth century there was in excess of 100 tons with François I who had to pay his army no longer raised through his barons and their vassals. Between 1629 and 1650, the tax went up steeply from 400 to 1000 tons. The wars of the Fronde followed. Louis XIV and his successors were forced to be more careful and fiscal pressure declined in France throughout the eighteenth century in sharp contrast to England where taxes were higher because of the parliamentary system. As a comparison, let us remember that America exported from 1501 to 1600 approximately 25,000 tons of quality silver or in other words an average of 250 tons per year with large fluctuations. Hence at the start of the fourteenth century the impact of royal taxes. It made for the penetration of currency in daily life almost, throughout the whole kingdom, even though a system of barter did continue. France was not the whole of the Christian world, however it did amount to over a quarter in terms of population. It was preponderant on the continent. The king was expensive, yet internal peace and the rule of law were invaluable. Inside France and elsewhere this was appreciated. The population did not feel that the high level of security the monarchy brought to their lives was too expensive.

This point seems clear that the most important factor for the monetarization of society was not due to fairs nor the *colleganza*, nor letters of exchange (nor even the advent of credit facilities which will be dealt with by others), but to royal tax which brought about that of feudal rents to be paid the landed nobility. Payment in toil and part-payment in kind were psychologically devalued in contrast to money. These small coins that every year each tenant farmer had to procure in order to gain freedom and security had a greater impact on change than the great arabesques of commerce. It was this meagre money, more copper than precious metal, money that was painfully earned, (almost wrenched from an invisible "cerro de Potosi"), unremarkable, product of the glebe and working hands, that was amassed and weighed more than the imports from the Americas and Asia put together on the great trading exchanges of Antwerp, Sevilla, Lisbon, Genoa and later Amsterdam and London.

The expenditure of the king of France, collected every year, taken from the agricultural labor and various crafts that go with farming (which until the seventeenth century was worth the whole expenditure of all Christian kings apart from Spain for a while) were like another American continent, older and more dependable, more regular than the wealth of the Zacatecas, Potosi or even later Ouro Preto or the Minas Gerais.

We could look at the terminology. In Latin what we call money is directly linked to livestock. The English say money; the Germans "*Geld*"; the Spanish "*dinero*." The French are the only ones to link the precious metal with the monetary reality (*argent*—silver but also money). Spain which mined the largest silver mines (Zacatecas, Potosi etc.) do not confuse *dinero* with *plata*. Quevedo writes that Mr. Money is a powerful person. This French uniqueness shows the longevity and permanency of Charlemagne's silver currency to that of the five franc piece (the *thune*). This confusion shows the profoundly peasant nature of the kingdom with its silver and copper coins that have been accumulated with such hardship to give to the tax collector who is hated but necessary since without him the Fleur de Lys (French Royal emblem) would cease to be able to protect the land. The thirty coins that Judas Iscariot received for betraying the divine Master were silver.

Metal is sterile. Metal is wealth but a static and false wealth. It is a redundant value that represents the true values: productivity, consumption and exchange, which are better symbolized in a more abstract way with paper which is no more than a sign. A silver coin is sterile and when buried, as the scholastic theologian would tell you, it will not bear fruit. This money, peasant money, royal money, the money of the state is also the usurers' money. Note how usage and the word itself in French is not well suited to the transition from usury to interest.

There is a gulf separating the Europe of Calvin's letter on usury and the Catholic practice of unredeemable rent together with the letter that can only be preserved by risk-taking, a gulf that show in the vocabulary. The refusal to consider any interest that is not perpetual or one that might be associated with risk comes from a psychological block that is the product of a century-old experience.

Money needs to be rehabilitated by removing it from the association with usury and the iron collar of the state. Despite praiseworthy efforts (think of Urba) there is still a long way to go. Money for us still smells of thesaurization (the exemption of works of art from wealth tax) and the mausoleum of the king (the Pyramids of Cheops, through to Versailles, The Bastille Opera and the Tres Grande Bibliotheque).

Money is not a monster but accompanies, as I think has been shown, an exchange, therefore it means communication, the written language, a subtle, creative thought process. It seems to me that the correlations that I have tried to establish prove this. There is no greater act of folly known to modern history than the simply backward and murderous measure taken by the Bolsheviks (Leninists) in the autumn of 1918 when they abolished money. It killed many more than the secret police and as many as the war. Money is on the side of reason in the widest and most objective sense of the word.

A final proof, perhaps from the correlations that you yourself have made, the most significant innovations in monetary techniques took place before or after the discovery of the Americas. Taxes in the fourteenth century and increased foreign trade, the "frontiers" in the Anglo-Saxon sense of the word (as used by Frederick Jackson Turner), operate as catalysts for the rule of acquisitions. America and the inflationary upsurge of the sixteenth century (times 5) were an overflowing river. There was invasion of territory, however the sixteenth century in terms of financial techniques, and monetary developments made few improvements. Creative ingenuity manifested itself earlier, in the Italian Middle Ages or later (Lowlands, Holland and England with the extension of credit facilities). America was discovered and exploited through the stern-post (1200), the caravel (sixteenth century), Marteloggio's tables (fourteenth century), the letters of exchange (13th-14th centuries) and a far older *colleganza*, plus through the use of the compass as devised by Peter de Marecourt in the thirteenth century. A second creative wave took place afterwards. Others will explain it.

As a product of the mind and the thirst for outside experiences, money does not exist. Only the mind which created in the first place, really exists and cannot refrain from creating further forms or it would wither. Those who declare that history has come to an end are making a serious mistake. History like life itself goes on.

The Promise of Money and a Return to the Golden Age: A Financial Revolution and Hope of Enlightenment

Jean-Marie Thiveaud

"The Golden Age of the human race is not in the past but awaiting us in the perfection of the social order: our forebears did not see it, but our children will one day get there, and it is up to us to prepare the way."

This is the conclusion of a small treatise, "Of the Reorganisation of European Society" that Count Henri de Saint-Simon and Augustin Thierry, his disciple, delivered to those nations meeting at the Congress of Vienna, in October 1814.

This proclamation, which heralds in the new era of industry and progress sums up the militant optimism of the preceding century when Europe in the age of Enlightenment wished, in the name of reason, above all to reconcile money and happiness, when financiers and scientists entrusted the fate of the world to money.

The passion for freedom possessing a world enslaved in the snares of the gods and time, the belief in reason and science, a greedy optimism for universal happiness, the dream of heaven on earth, always—and even above all—as if experimentally, had a financial manifestation.

The "financial revolution" that transformed England in the first half of the eighteenth century, which would soon spread throughout Europe of the Enlightenment, prepared the way for the social and political revolutions of the last decade, carried as every revolution on utopian flights of fancy. In the Wealth of Nations by Adam Smith who speaks only briefly of finance, singles out credit as the wings of Icarus of the economy.

Taking up, from amongst so many definitions of utopia, that given by Jean-Marie Domenach some 15 years ago: "sense in imagination," it seems to me that the financial revolution of the Enlightenment rather shows the power of imagination in reasoning.

This financial revolution had various faces that effectively followed and crossed each other's paths: credit revolution, technical revolution, provident companies, savings and insurance revolutions, which I will try and outline.

Fed by the energy of the Enlightenment, these ideological or technical changes were ultimately founded in the crucible of social and political upheavals, later purified in the fire of revolutionary wars to feed the bright hopes of the next century. Yet as could be expected and in keeping with the way of utopias, they left positive marks and set in place for a long time after the financial structures that still exists to the present day. The utopian dreams speedily gave, from the start of the eighteenth century, the financial world an esoteric tone that still reverberates in contemporary spheres and circles even 200 years later.

Towards the end of the seventeenth century and the beginning of the eighteenth century, almost all Europeans states were paralysed by what liberal economists of the end of the nineteenth century call the "wholesale debt" of civilised nations.

This increase of national debt can essentially be explained by the many conflicts that punctuated the century, "gentlemen's wars" that in size and intensity were very costly. This general insolvency upset the financial organization of the countries involved, and the accumulated debt led to systematic borrowing and in order to continue to borrow, the states needed to regularly service the repayment of their debt. Paradoxically, yet in a dynamic way, the needs of the state to borrow increased due to the philosophical quest for the happiness of mankind and all the avidly universal scientific hopes that everywhere fermented in Europe over this period.

The war economy and the increasing financial disruption of state institutions awaken in those who nevertheless benefited most, bankers and publicists, the mobilizing dream of universal prosperity and everlasting peace.

Maybe never in the history of the modern era have so many people, coming from many walks of life and countries, gathered together to effectively combine advances in science and finance, improve social morality, introduce fair political systems, improve the lot of the poor and allow for growth in public and private wealth.

Together with the parallel development of trade and the first spurt of industrial growth, both inextricably linked to the war effort, the financial needs of the belligerent nations sparked off the first revolution of credit.

Credit which would become in the following century the guiding star for progress in the industrial age painfully began its ascent at the dawn of the eighteenth century. Its trajectory which for some time was erratic fascinated every nation who prior to or after Adam Smith, saw growth in their wealth as the key to social order based henceforth on the economy.

In France and England especially, tax returns due both to the slowness in collection and the cost of collecting were not sufficient for the ordinary needs of the state even in peace time. It was inevitable that they should have to borrow periodically. The sovereign had, since the seventeenth century the mathematical tools (for political arithmetics) to foresee their future income and calculate temporary loans that might perpetuate themselves. Yet each state needed to widen its credit base in order to dispose more effectively and economically of those resources that it had at its disposal. The first hurdle that states had to overcome was the system of loans underwritten by investors (also called partisans or financiers and similar, *similia similibus,* to modern institutional investors) yet turning to public subscription would not yield vast returns. Every country needed to have an effective credit system which implied the organisation of a financial market supported by sound institutions and with a suitable mechanism in place.

Each country also needed to be able to manage the paying off of the national debt, the risk of partial or total bankruptcy being so great under the weight of debt whose growth threatens social and public order. The repeated going back on promises, most particularly in France (Chamfort, in order to add spice to his maxims, outlines about 15 examples over the century) emphasized the shambles of a state that had neither the necessary resources nor political know-how to solve this problem.

Also they had to protect themselves from what modern-day financiers would refer to as a systemic risk: the quantity of public borrowing could not increase indefinitely without a huge amount of productive capital being used which rapidly would result in disaster for the economy of the country. However familiar methods of paying off the debt, through budget endowment, increased the tax burden.

The necessity of keeping a balance between the national debt and the national economy led therefore to the organisation of national credit, the creation of institutions capable of building up reserves, to receive the citizens' savings, and stimulate trade and circulation of money. Each country tried in their own way, depending on their culture, their political and economic structures, to address these questions.

France and England at the same time needed to find solutions to the problems raised by their continually being at war and their respective course gave rise to differing models that would develop at different rates, fast in England and very slowly in France.

From its creation in 1694, the Bank of England brilliantly ushered in the credit revolution. It quickly established a reputation as the most powerful credit organisation in the history of mankind. It started with a war loan and the bill laid before Parliament by Lord Montague was voted without much apparent interest. The *Act of Tonnage* that made the Bank authorised a loan of 1,500,000 pounds which the Bank and the government immediately launched. An initial capital of 1.2 million was formed by City bankers which was then placed at the disposal of the state, which in turn gave a high interest of 8% to the subscribers. This first operation on the relief of the public debt is no doubt one of the reasons why the Bank of England did so well, the results of which were readily visible on the financial markets. It rapidly brought down interest rates with the price of money going from 20-30% at the end of the seventeenth century to 4.5% or 5% in the first decade of the next century. This improved rate immediately had a beneficial effect of state finances and debt. The English government could therefore borrow over the following century at an average rate of 3% with the Bank operating a virtually continuous conversion of the national debt.

The direct role of the Bank on redemption was strengthened in 1716 with the creation of the first *Sinking Fund* which had all the appearances of direct management of the national debt by government. In reality, the English Treasury limited itself to routine accounting whereas the Bank managed and operated the fund.

The Bank in turn replaced the Treasury in issuing titles of national assets, managed public borrowing and in this also fulfilled the function of a savings account.

It was of course also a central bank and did all the ordinary operations of a bank: discount, letters of exchange, issuing of notes, etc. It was effective since a proportion of the state's borrowing, paid directly by the bank, went back to it after and this closed-circuit allowed it in times of crisis to withstand shocks.

The English model, similar to the national political structure that William of Orange set up at the same time, is summed up by the Bank, a symbol of the alliance between the state and capital, between the Exchequer and the City Bankers. Finance or money became the symbolic reference of the new Parliamentary monarchy replacing the stock of signs of divine right of the old monarchy which they had gradually lost. In many ways this revolutionary institution thus was a channel linking capital involved in the national debt and the everyday needs of the national economy. It established a balance between short-term needs and long term reserves that give stability, and felicitously reconciled, with seeming impartiality, individual interest and the demands of the state. The Bank of England represents a fabulous illustration of the classical logic of finance and the state, money and the people, which was embodied by the former Roman *census*.

It was a striking example of a self-governing financial conjuring trick. A frightfully efficient institution providing a climate of confidence within the country, offering other nations a picture of "unlimited credit"—that secret weapon which is still talked about in European monetary discussions.

In 1716, the very same year that England set up the first *Sinking Fund* between the Bank and the Exchequer, John Law a Scotsman came to Regency France and inaugurated the foundations of the first structures of modern credit: the Law system although a failure, was a fabulous precursor and origin of a rich line of successors. From its very inception, and right until the end of this short and dramatic adventure the principal idea of the system, of the General Bank, was the redemption of a huge National debt which in his last years Louis XIV had left behind. The urgency of this task goes some way in explaining the total support of the regent. John Law perceived that healthy public finance was linked to economic prosperity and vice-versa. Thus, his system was based on a form of "perpetual motion" which expressed, in terms of the fluctuation of finance, the then vague idea of an economic circuit. This interaction cunningly spotted by Law drew him into huge experiments that rapidly exceeded the sole objective of managing the debt with a confusion of public borrowing and the shares of commercial companies. Law became entangled in redemption, mixing up short-term deposits with long-term ones and ignoring the need for different ways of handling them. The state debt which is often long-term, sometimes even perpetual, necessitates on the part of the recipient constant attention in order to avoid crises and fluctuation. On the other hand, how would it be possible to base state finances on a sound footing with commercial enterprises that belong to the world of risk and are short-term propositions? John Law, despite his ingenious inventions, despite his astounding premonitions, confused both role, one that of the general depository on the model of the Bank of England and the other the monopolists businessmen, the king's money and that of the many subscribers and depositors.

Even so, John Law no doubt brought in terms of public finance some novel propositions which would be used for a long time after and also despite the incredible failure of his enterprise. Besides, or even instead of a heavy tax apparatus, Law built up a bank so as to get rid of all sorts of taxes, a universal business and a general system. Thus based on financial circuits the system should have become the basis for a political and economic solidarity that would merge individual and public interest. The state would no longer be spendthrift but would direct credit and the economy through the control of the General Bank and the India Company.

The Bank, guaranteed by the state, "is in reality," writes Law, "an established treasury that serves as a deposit for the King, for the people and for foreigners, yet access to this public account is always freely given and the king has no real call nor interest in halting its circulation."

Although the Bank of England was more effective in bringing about this credit revolution, Law's system was as important in its effect or even more important since it founded in the realm of ideas and fed the over-riding power of the imagination. Law's system despite and because of its failure, marked in French society the dawning of the dream of wealth for everyone. He interpreted to a wondering audience the fairy tale magic of this revolutionary notion of credit. Credit is a mirage—"all the nation is taking part in the fantastical search for Ithaca," Henry Baudrillard wrote around 1880. John Law waved in front of the people the *tempting golden branch*: the bank note; he revealed and shared the grand design of all alchemists succeeding in changing paper into gold and vice versa.

Credit then became an ideal widespread practice of utopia, the El Dorado of the Renaissance which henceforth was open to all, on the banks of the Mississippi. Money has a big shortcoming, it has to be earned; credit allows for easy wealth. France in this period was a society of gamblers who willingly confused the lottery and the bank as is borne out by the thoughts of Duc de Saint-Simon, Henri's great-uncle. Princes, peers of the realm, the whole nobility, saw an easy escape from the widespread poverty that went with the fortunes of war and were quick to swap their "glorious share" of old against the new shares of Law's bank.

"The speedy revolution of fortunes also took place in the minds," writes a witness, Duclos in his memoirs of the Regency. "Prior to this time, that can be called fabulous, individuals could only hope to make a fortune through toil and thrift.... Today people no longer set limits to their desires."

This sublimely poetical work, dedicated by John Law to France, also reminds one of other classical poems. Leon Bloy at the end of the nineteenth century portrays France of the Enlightenment where the Bucolics of Moloch were feted and in fact the myth of a golden age, sung by Virgil and Ovid, found its ephemeral reality in the streets of Paris. The period seemed to announce prosperity and harmony for all. Many had a share in it for their sins or profit and not everybody took refuge in wiping it off their memory.

This enterprising portent of the golden age, credit, was also appeared as a leveler of social inequalities and an old Liberal like Baudrillard, in the first years of the Third Republic drew this conclusion from Law's experiment: "The scope of this system can be measured not only in social but socialist terms."

Andre Delaporte's thesis on the idea of equality during the age of the Enlightenment found in the financial field a close and functional correspondence with the political and literary ideas expressed at the time.

No doubt the failure of Law and its momentous consequences would haunt the memories and consciences of the meekest for many decades after. "We see so many people get rich and poor so quickly." Duclos also wrote "that one would think, often correctly, that we can place our hope for gain or fear loss in all these sudden revolutions in state finances." This popular fear was also shadowed by a clearly political fear of the enormous threat that such a system presented for an absolute monarchy with its divine right of kings. Although the magical benefits of credit remained more or less understood and acceptable for the French, they would have to wait for the fall of the Ancien Regime to give themselves institutions that for decades had been enriching other countries.

Reports, often tinged with envy, bear witness to the financial success of the hereditary enemy next-door. Yet the Bank of England and the Parliamentary Monarchy were also frequently denounced. Inversely and side by side, those reformers who were eager for a constitution were, since Montesquieu, the very same who advocated financial innovation, praising the benefits of debt redemption and looking to the mechanisms of public credit to avert high taxes.

Following the fall of the system, the state and the financial world divorced in a typically French way, the opposite of the objective alliance that joined the English government and the capitalists in the City of London. Other countries would remain fascinated by the magic-like promises of credit and for me Russia is the most telling example of the rule of an idea at least in terms of financial questions. Legend tells that Peter the Great offered John Law his carriage to run away and join him. The Tsar is also said to have suggested that he built a town in the Empire entirely devoted to finance. Law preferred the Venetian gambling tables, yet Russian governments right up to Catherine II were enthusiastic over Law's experiments and were to continue them. They built, with many false starts, a number of financial and monetary institutions that were totally breathtaking and which, to the present-day, observers see as a Wonderland through the looking glass, yet with the benefit of two century's hindsight and faced with the plight of the last few years, this vision seems wholly vindicated.

The failure of Law's system set in place a sort of divide in eighteenth century financial Europe, isolating France and its allies from the monetary trade that was developing in the Northern European countries. The physiocrats of the middle of the century continued to scorn financial companies and merchants. Their ideas on credit remained very limited and Quesnay who was against it denounced "the trade in money through commercial paper and the bankers who have no allegiance to king or country."

The cosmopolitan attitude of those involved in finance, praised by Voltaire and criticized by Rousseau, was a common argument right up until the revolutionary years and "patriots" were quick to dismiss the world of bankers who knew no borders. When, during the last quarter of the eighteenth century, Turgot attempted to launch a new policy of credit, he had to rely on a Swiss, Panchaud, and a Scotsman, Clonard, to set up the Deposit Account. This institution, authorized in 1776, which is rather far-fetchedly seen as the ancestor of the Bank of France, was not invested with the missionary ideals of a great credit institution such as the Bank of England. After an initial success, it quickly ran out of steam due to its complicated dealings with the state. The needs of the Treasury, monetary variations and the fluctuations of the interest rates resulted, from 1783, in successive crises which led to speculative dealing and an outcry among political and financial opponents of the regime. Mirabeau, Claviere or Brissot were particularly fierce in their attacks on the Deposit Account which they saw as the root of all this speculation.

The century ended with France split between Voltaire's position of: "The rich are born to spend a lot, the poor are made to save a lot..." and the views of the philosophical economists summed up by the moralizing radicalism of Rousseau: "Those who manipulate money soon learn to misappropriate it..."; and furthermore: "Make money an object of scorn and if possible useless." Sebastien Mercier's heated words in 1788, despite his position as a well-known utopist, expressed fully the opposition of a section of public opinion: "Speculators lack any patriotic feeling; they are foreign bodies inside the nation who only know how to hide their money and through agile maneuvering they give birth to imaginary creations."

Over these same years, public credit, which the French economists of the Enlightenment held that it had no influence of national prosperity, became a cornerstone of the political system and one of the main arguments at the start of the revolution that the enlightened bankers sparked off. Senac de Meilhan, a shrewd regional governor (*intendant*), a clever economist who later emigrated, wrote in 1790 that "bankers are citizens of every country and the republican regime was the most suitable to people whose wealth was available, who, being divorced from the social hierarchy only exist through their wealth and whose only ambition is to increase it."

The second indicator of the great financial revolution of the century took place in the field of technique.

The influence of the Enlightenment in the 1730-50's and even more so in the three decades of the eighteenth century was practically felt in the great increase in financial innovation. The dual flow of philosophy and mathematics ignited what I have called the "actuarial utopia" whose efficient fervour would totally transform the financial scene and set up the foundations for systems which still exist today. Dynamic international debate concerned not only on public finance but also in the sphere of private individual trade in an atmosphere of cooperation or diversity that might be imitated in our present discussions.

The enormous steps forward in financial techniques that were evident in the furthest reaches of Europe can easily be explained by the need already mentioned, yet at the same time they aimed at a goal that was more ambitious and nobler, the reform of state and society. This sort of ambiguity of objective might seem surprising today but it was characteristic of the period. Thus Deparcieux's work on rates of mortality, like many initial demographic studies, had as its prime objective the improvement of some financial product or other, even though these studies had other obvious uses for the public administration or improvement of health. Progress in calculating probabilities was fired by a similar wish for financial efficiency as was conceived by scholars such as Condorcet.

A real need to resolve these pressing questions set within a larger debate in which both God and Man, figures and time were implicated lent itself to a concerted attempt at reaching universal happiness. The physiocrats who scorned money paradoxically gave the financial utopians their best slogan. "The greatest happiness to the greatest number" became the goal, already within their grasp, of social, economic and political reformers.

The difficulties that most states were experiencing: debt nearing bankruptcy, excessive private speculation and speculation in financial circles, the anarchy that reigned in the handling of goods and interest rates that demanded, for the sake of efficiency and morality, a rationalisation of methods and machinery.

Scholars, lawyers, philosophers and mathematicians rallied to the task or were mobilized by state financiers and private bankers to add their weight to an international attempt to regulate and clean up trade. Contributors were legion and from every country in Europe; the English were fired by the Germans prior to enriching French thinking and the Dutch or the Italians; ideas flew around and each shared with the other their theories and projects.

Thus as well as the idea of equality, carried most especially on the chimeric wings of credit, was added in the name of mathematics and in more concrete ways, the demand for moral and financial equity. The ethics of the Enlightenment meant that in terms of borrowing, neither lender nor borrower should be wronged. The state therefore was singled out in every country for juggling with rates of interest, exchange and the impossible repayment of their mammoth debts. This detailed and difficult reflection on public debt also, carried on the philosophical verve of the Enlightenment, meant that they cast a look at the economy, the social order and political constitutions. The principle of debt itself, to the classical world, was at the roots of ancient laws and presided over the birth of the contract. In this period, with its nostalgic dream of primitive democratic societies, the powerful orators and manipulators would invoke public faith, the confidence that bonds the people and is expected by the people of the state.

Mathematicians allied themselves with philosophers and lawyers to find remedies for the national debt and by introducing the concept of rational equity in financial affairs they built up the theory of social contract, founded on a contractual relationship, involving sums of money, financially effective, between members of a society. They introduced on the national stage, with a mathematical stroke, a new economic factor: the people who would become a statistical unit of measure, accountable, producing wealth, valued, masters of their own destiny and able to brave the future.

Europe soon would appear like a vast laboratory of financial innovation, where the prosaic needs of the marketplace encounters the preference of the Enlightenment for applied mathematics. Thus, especially in the middle of the century, the means of public borrowing were used as a starting point for many studies that from Hally and Deparcieux to Price and Condorcet, would transform not only scientific knowledge but also the very structures of society. The work of Price, Fatio, Saint-Cyran, Laplace and Condorcet for instance which renewed the field of combined interest and the calculation of probability, were primarily motivated by the search for a winning formula capable of feeding the increasingly prickly and unyielding field of life annuity.

All these scientific theories, applied to finance, play a part in the great philosophical currents of the time, shared by both bankers and scholars. One explains the other in a period when, as with frontiers, barriers of thought, disciplines and ways of expressing oneself did not exist. Basically the technical problems of life annuities which revealed their variety, the long-term and the uncertainty of accident, was nothing more than transposing the great debate of the Enlightenment with its freeing of humanity, the final ends of history and the freedom of responsibility of Man before his destiny, into concrete terms. The introduction, brought about by mathematics, of the idea of a cycle of life and the first experiments of pensions and insurance has its philosophical and universal corollary in the metaphor much-loved by Kant, Lessing, Herder and many others of the ages of man, which transforms historical perspective and sets up the notion of progress which Condorcet would enthuse over.

An international debate began, which over the century founded, against the tenets of the physiocrats, what we would today call a real financial economy, yet already parallel to the real economy, already marked with the seal of fiction characterizing, in the late stages of the twentieth century, financial bubbles and spheres.

The practical applications were energetically developed in Holland, Germany and England, whereas in France they remained buried in the hearts of various clans in the form of hopes. The political group that in the 1780's brought together numerous bankers such as Panchaud, Delessert and Claviere for example and publicists and scholars such as Mirabeau, Brissot, Condorcet or Talleyrand would rapidly be carried away by the revolutionary events. Yet their theories and institutional projects, supported by science and techniques, inspired by the wish for democratic well-being, nevertheless would become reality for their descendants and successors in the next century through the combined and paradoxical actions of the restoration governments and romantic socialism.

But the technical revolution was closely and effectively linked to a further manifestation of financial revolution, stronger than any other utopian dream, the provident revolution.

This revolution, in a way ideal and utopian, seems to me to be more important in its consequences than the political revolutions that its fed. A revolutionary idea, providence affects equally the institution of public finances, the banking world, the role of the state and the organisation of society. It of course was a product of the philosophical and scientific revolutions of the century, from Newton to Kant, Leibniz, Lessing and Herder, up to Laplace and Condorcet, yet it had its embodiment in the financial world. It followed faithfully the development of techniques, especially in the field already mentioned of life annuity, through the lure of composite interest rates and the incantation of probabilities.

All products—annuities, *tontines* and life interests—in fact were accompanied by an interest rate that in the eighteenth century became the main preoccupation of financiers. The intellectual fascination of Europe of the Enlightenment with composite interest over straightforward interest marked the transition from a period of discontinuity to one of continuity and inaugurates the organisation of a defined limited period of time with at least two temporal moments and leading to a necessary projection of gain in a measurable future. Composite interest also needed a more developed and equitable credit system since it was obviously based on accurate calculation.

Several countries became aware of the benefit of a public savings institution like that of England. Portugal and Russia created deposit accounts whilst absolutist France left this project in abeyance until the restoration.

These technical considerations had an influence on law and morality not least since they seemed virtuous alternatives to the old excesses of usury and even more because with life income there is a wager on a sacred element: a human life and with a calculation of probability contests the old notion of fate. Bringing the cycle of life into a temporal representation without a doubt was one of the most important achievements of the century of Enlightenment, and even more so as it manifested itself concretely in the solution to burning financial problems. Mortality studies were supported and spurred on by bankers; they also encouraged the quantifying of risk and the refining of probability calculations to ceaselessly improve the return on life incomes. In turn the philosophers promised, using mathematical proof, control of Man's future and philanthropic financiers invented the first pension systems to guard against old-age.

Governments were also involved in this speculation which provided them with a way of managing the national debt. The geometrical progress of composite interest allowed to believe in an arithmetic redemption of their incredible debts.

In real terms the projects and models became more numerous in France, England, Russia and Germany where clever mixes were devised for life incomes techniques, the national debt, composite interest rates and old-age pensions.

Thus Europe of the Enlightenment, and especially France, enthusiastically nurtured this actuarial utopia which promised a marvelous future for humanity through the dual benefit of redemption and providence, sorting out both or at the same time the problem of public credit and on the other hand the financial security of individuals up to their death. The social contract, which derives from mathematical and financial calculations, brings to the central stage, facing the people, in the hope of happiness and prosperity, a further actor, the state invested with god-like powers.

These technical-commercial [illegible] had an influence on law and morals, and at least since they seemed virtually [illegible] to the old exercise of usury, and even more because [illegible] a sacred [illegible] life and with [illegible] calculation of probability conflicted [illegible] the old notion of fate [illegible] into [illegible] without a doubt [illegible] of the most important achievements of the century [illegible] and even more [illegible] itself [illegible] to [illegible] changing [illegible]. Moreover [illegible] they also encouraged the [illegible] and the [illegible] of probability calculations [illegible] in turn the philosophers [illegible] mathematicians [illegible] and philanthropic [illegible] invented [illegible].

Governments were also involved in this speculation which [illegible] them [illegible] the nations [illegible] progress of [illegible] interest [illegible] of them [illegible].

[illegible] France, England, [illegible] and Germany where [illegible] were devised for [illegible] interest rate [illegible].

The [illegible] of the [illegible], and especially France, enthusiastically [illegible] this [illegible] utopia which [illegible] towards [illegible] through the [illegible] public credit and [illegible] and the [illegible] social [illegible] stage [illegible] of happiness and prosperity [illegible].

FINANCIAL INSTABILITY: THE INTER-WAR EXPERIENCE

Marc Uzan

The inter-war period was unique in the history of international finance since it saw three very different monetary experiments: floating exchange rates from 1921-26, fixed exchange rates from 1927-31 and finally controlled exchange rate until the end of the 1930's. As with all transitional periods, the inter-war period is a very interesting period in the history of international finance. An analysis of this changing period will allow us to understand why Europe lost its financial power. Before the First World War, Britain was the strongest economic world power. London was the capital of international finance and the pound was the reference-point for the monetary system. In 1913 American growth was financed by capital coming from Europe. From being a debtor country before the First World War, it would change into world lender after the war.

This change in the configuration of the balance of payments had an immediate impact on various currencies. In fact the secretariat of the League of Nations saw the dollar as the international currency. The result of this change was that international trade was then calculated in dollars and no longer in pounds sterling. Hence the 1920's were years characterized by a break-up of spheres of influence. War and revolution had weakened the majority of European currencies. The Austro-Hungarian Empire was dismantled; the French franc which had been a symbol of stability lost a fifth of its value on the financial markets and in 1919, the German currency was worthless; the pound sterling, symbol of the power and financial hegemony of Britain and which before the war had been the key-stone of the gold standard, by 1919, was worth less than before the war.

The crisis of the 1930 would highlight the links between the international financial system and the world economy. The inter-war period was characterized by a period of badly managed hurried financial innovation against a backdrop of financial instability and a financial crisis with devastating macro-economic effects. This is why there is renewed interest in this period among American economists.

In this study, I would like to describe first of all the main developments of the financial markets between the two wars and work out how they link up with the macro-economic crisis of the 1930's. We will follow two paths. The first consists of describing the international financial balance following the First World War. The second will analyze more especially the various aspects of monetary instability over the inter-war period.

THE INTERNATIONAL FINANCIAL BALANCE AFTER THE FIRST WORLD WAR

The First World War unleashed forces that defined financial relations over the decade. One of the fist effects of the war was to change financial relations on the international markets. The United States changed from being a debtor nation to that of lender. Estimates show that in order to pay for the war 60% of American stocks and shares held by foreigners were sold to American investors between 1915 and 1916; between 1915 and 1919, more than 12 billion dollars of credit was given to the Allies by the United States. The European belligerents came out of the war with a huge foreign debt in favour of the United States. Towards the middle of the 1920's most of the countries had negotiated a repayment plan for their war loans. Between 1926 and 1931, the United States received almost 1 billion dollars in interest payments and repayment of capital.

German reparations also increased this flow of capital. The list of reparations established in London in 1921 was rescheduled as part of the arrangements of the Dawes Plan in 1924. The annuities demanded from Germany as part of this plan were paid on time until 1929. The Allies received from Germany almost 2 billion during the preceding five years.

Neither Germany nor the Allies were in a position to increase their exports in a corresponding proportion to the billions of dollars in exchange. If they had been capable of it, the other countries would probably not have been able to absorb further imports. The balance of international finance needed the United States and to a lesser extent Britain to recycle this flow of capital generated by the payment of reparations and interest. In fact the problem of recycling was much greater. The French, German and Belgium economies had been ravaged by war. Foreign credit was necessary to import basic consumer goods and to finance economic reconstruction. The partitioning of central and eastern Europe into half a dozen sovereign states had splintered industries and transport systems. The huge investments in infrastructure, materials and equipment increased the demand for foreign capital. For the United States who had traditionally been an importer of capital, the logical solution was to start to export their capital towards Europe.

Initially, New York supplied capital in the form of short term loans, mainly trade credits by way of London. The largest export of American capital in the inter-war years took place between 1919 and 1920. Yet from the time when European governments asked for capital intended for long-term projects and not just for the import of consumer goods, commercial credits were insufficient. Commercial banks had already begun to open agencies abroad. Their representatives competed fiercely for foreign loans. The banks opened branches in the United States to sell foreign securities. They opened their doors to investors who were used to the advantages of foreign values which had been produced by the *Liberty Loan Act* between 1917 and 1919.

Foreign loans during the 1920's never reached the height of those in pre-war years. From 1902 to 1913, the absolute value of sales of current accounts of the nine industrialized nations had reached an average of 4% of the GNP. Between 1925 and 1928, the same indicators were at 1.4%

The structural changes were much more pronounced in the international monetary circles. The First World War had seen the end of the age of the gold standard. The international monetary system was rebuilt in the following decade. By the end of the war the United States was the only country left that could convert gold. The dollar became the standard currency. Of all the currencies it was the only one that retained its pre-war value. This was why the dollar became the point of reference for the stabilizing of the other currencies. This was a very important fact that would underline the growing role of American monetary policy in the rest of the world. The first countries that reestablished the pegging of their currencies to gold were those that had suffered from hyper-inflation as a result of the war; Austria in 1923; Germany in 1924; Hungary in 1925; France in 1926 and Italy in 1927.

By 1927 the reconstruction of the gold standard was complete. This new gold standard was very different to its predecessor. The gold pieces that had been in circulation were concentrated in the reserves of central banks. Almost all of these were authorized by law to hold part of the endorsed guarantees in convertible currency rather than gold.

The major nations that had reserves in currencies, the United States and Great Britain, continued to hold mainly gold, while the other central banks kept part of their international reserves in the form of credit in London or New York. Even though this practice had been usual prior to the First World War it had not been so widespread nor so official. Before the war only three countries—Russia, Japan and India—had kept most of their stocks in currency. Now most of the central banks kept a part of their stock in the form of banknotes. Worldwide the proportion of banknotes had probably doubled since 1913, to which was added a growing diversity of currencies. Before 1913 the majority of reserves were expressed in banknotes and were found in London. With the rise of the dollar as the dominant currency European currencies could no longer form the bulk of a portfolio. Often the central banks had a varied portfolio of pounds, dollars, francs and other currencies the make-up of which would vary depending on the circumstances.

This in brief was the financial and monetary system as it stood on the brink of the crisis. The following ten years showed its shortcomings and would prove how chronically unstable it was. Loss of confidence in money and financial institutions would complete this disintegration.

The Collapse of the Financial System and Loss of Confidence in Money

Historians of the Great Crisis emphasize the part played by the Wall Street among the various causes of the collapse of the financial system. Yet, to understand the relationship between the monetary system and the crisis, one has to go back to 1928. This was when the American central bank, preoccupied by financial speculation which had reached an intolerable level, started to raise interest rates. Five quarters later, such efforts had managed to reduce speculation and restored public confidence in liquid assets. Yet this rise in rates would restrict loans in the economy. As the price of money from day to day was increasing to unprecedented heights, it suddenly seemed surer and more profitable for American investors to wait and keep their money liquid. Loan portfolios went down rapidly: 1 billion dollars in 1927 and 700 million in 1928. This decline resulted in European countries having problems in meeting payments for their foreign debt. Towards the end of 1928 Germany was clearly in recession.

But following the financial crash, the Federal Reserve did not hesitate in putting into circulation additional notes. To avoid the sale of shares and the collapse of financial brokers in the last months of 1929 the central bank injected credit. By October and November 1929 federal banks' American shares had doubled. For the people, the financial crash heralded a new era of uncertainty. Worried families refrained from buying consumer products. There was a fall in spending on cars, for example, which got worse after 1929.

The change of the monetary policy of the central bank coincided with the first financial crisis at the end of 1930. It was less serious than the second in October 1931 or the third in March 1933. The instability of the banking system was a global phenomenon. Bankruptcies were common in 1931 in Austria, Germany and Hungary and in 1932 in Sweden and Belgium in 1933.

The collapse of prices of agricultural produce undermined the profits of the rural banks. The fall in industrial production reduced the bank results in Germany and Austria. Fraud and embezzlement had a large part to play in the Swedish example in 1932. The only common factor in all these crises was the role of the gold standard. The problems of the banking system led central banks to intervene, lending as a last resort. The monetary authorities were forced to discount assets on account of intermediaries who were plagued by a hemorrhage on savings accounts. However the need to be able to convert into gold forced the central banks to have a minimum amount of gold and currencies available to pay debts. The system hindered the central banks from providing additional assets to contain the crisis within the banking system. For example in July 1931, at the height of the German banking crisis, the size of the Reichsbank's reserves fell to the 40% fixed ceiling, below which it risked violating the gold standard rule. Thus the Reichsbank could only take provisional steps to prop up the banking system which sapped confidence in future convertibility and provoked a run on international reserves. The Reichsbank was forced, in order to end this, to set up a foreign exchange limit.

If the instability of the banking system could shake confidence in the gold standard, the opposite was also true. The clearest example was the American crisis of March-April 1933. Anticipation of a devaluation of the dollar was the most important factor that led to a general banking crisis. It was known that Franklin Roosevelt the president of the United States was in favour of the devaluation of the dollar. Congress was on the contrary in favour of an over-valuation and passed the Wheeler and Thomas amendments. Anticipating its devaluation savers withdrew their money and converted it into gold and cash. Uncertainty over the convertibility of the dollar provoked a rush of withdrawals of money from the banks by the savers.

In Austria, the 1931 crisis started in the banking system. Confidence was destroyed by revelations of the extent of bank loans by the Kredit Anstalt bank. The central bank gave additional liquidities to the banking system; the issuing of notes grew at 23% in the first months.

Cover for the issuing of currency was no longer assured by the gold stock which reinforced fears over the parity with gold. Savers who were no longer willing to take the risk hurried to withdraw their money from the banking system, and changed them into other currencies to avoid losses due to devaluation.

The more central banks quickly injected assets the more the loss of confidence in the money spread. The lenders intervened decisively in the system in an anti-productive way. The interwoven nature of the banking system and the peculiar structure of the gold standard meant that financial instability crossed from one country to the next. When Great Britain was forced to devalue in September 1931, the impact was felt directly by the dollar. The fact that one of the safe currencies had been devalued cast doubt on the others. A speculative onslaught on the dollar was the inevitable consequence. The central banks liquidated their foreign notes and transformed them into gold. The proportion of bank-notes for international provision fell by 2/3rds between the end of 1929 and the end of 1931. The value of available reserves to cover monetary commitments declined sharply. Pressure on those countries that were part of the gold standard intensified.

In the same way as with convertibility crises so the banking panic proved contagious. The German Banks had kept a part of their operations in Vienna. The Austrian banks had done the same with Berlin. The rush on the Austrian banks led to a withdrawal of their deposits, displacing pressure onto the German banking system. When the Austrian government reacted to this crisis by imposing exchange controls, fear that Germany might react in the same way led to other depositors closing their accounts in Berlin.

Via this mechanism, the crisis spread from one country to another. Through various different channels, the banking crisis was having an effect on economic activity.

The banking panic forced savers to withdraw their deposits and buy notes which reduced the supply of money and making prices fall. The decline of stocks discouraged expenditure through its effects on interest rates. More importantly was the deflationary effect of the fall in prices. Deflation raises the real weight of the credits needed to be recovered reinforcing the vulnerability of debtors to bankruptcy, eroding the value of guarantees they could offer to their bankers. In many countries agricultural prices fell by 2/3rds, tripling the actual costs of agricultural mortgages and eliminating any possibility of financial credibility that farmers might have had.

The financial crisis also dislocated the provisions of financial services. The banks threatened by the flood of savers were not in a position to make risky investments in industry or trade. Small companies looking for money for running costs were unable to find any at whatever the rate. They therefore had to reduce their operation. Companies who had lucrative yet risky investments opportunities were unable to obtain the necessary finance to exploit them.

The collapse of average-term credit seems to have had a depressing effect on economic activity, without mentioning the effects of banking bankruptcies on financial provision. This effect spread outside the United States to Austria, Belgium, France, Germany, Hungary, Italy, Poland and Romania.

In 1933 Germany, the most debt-laden country in Europe suspended payment of the majority of its foreign bonds. Many small Latin American debtors did not have a choice. Some of the most indebted nations like Canada, Australia and Argentina faithfully continued to service their foreign debt. Yet these countries were the exception for non-payment was in general the case. Negotiations between debtors and creditors were to stretch over decades. Often part-servicing of the foreign debt was demanded, stopped and started once again. The general non-payment had a catastrophic impact on the capital market. American loans which had slowed down during the summer of 1928 rose once again after the Wall Street crash.

Before 1931, non-payment of debt alerted foreign investors to the risky nature of the enterprise. The debenture market was in the doldrums for the rest of the 1930's. The influx of foreign capital of average importance was in the form of trade credits and direct foreign investment.

Towards 1932, the situation deteriorated. The vast majority of borrowers had stopped the payment of their foreign debt. International loans had stopped working. Germany, Austria and Hungary had imposed foreign exchange controls and begun negotiations over compensation.

Great Britain in 1931 had been forced to withdraw from the gold standard and in the same year more than twenty other countries had followed suit. Bank bankruptcies were happening all over the place. Yet, the very financial worries, the loss of confidence in the role of the monetary authorities itself, paved a way out. The fall in international loans discouraged sovereign states from servicing their debts.

By suspending the servicing of their debts, they were able to redirect their resources towards internal uses. By transferring the interest of foreign accounts they improved the possibility of their payment. The need to reduce internal expenditure through imposing strict fiscal and monetary policies was largely avoided.

In those countries that had suspended servicing of their foreign debt, signs of recovery were seen in 1932. For governments more expansionist monetary policies were the main way of stimulating their economies. The end of the gold standard also gave them the freedom to pursue policies of growth. Convertibility was no longer a necessary requirement restricting central banks in offering money.

Yet, despite attempts to organize a coordinated reaction it was impossible to form any international cooperation. In the various countries governments analyzed differently the nature of the economic crisis. Being unsuccessful in diagnosing similarly the origin of the crisis, they were unable to agree on a coordinated course of action.

The devaluation of currencies and the stabilisation of internal prices ended the downward spiral of economic activity, for the same reasons that, in the preceding period, deflation had made the collapse worse.

The stabilisation or the slight increase in prices reversed the trend of the real costs of the work force. The actual pay slipped slightly thus encouraging employers to hire more people. Stable prices reversed the increasing impact of debts. Price rises, in national currency, of agricultural produce were especially important for agriculture. The stability of prices and provision of funds restored stability to the banking system.

Once rid of the gold standard, the banking authorities could act forcefully against the problems of the banking system. Banking crises were infrequent in those countries that were not part of the gold standard. When they did happen, as in Argentina in 1931, or else Sweden in 1932, the swift reaction of the authorities, free from the obligations of the gold standard, immediately halted the spread of the phenomenon.

Freed from the limits of the gold standard the countries might have re-launched their economies by increasing the quantity of money. However this was not the case. Voluntary restraint in monetary policy harked back to the financial disorder at the start of the 1920's, which was when the gold standard was last suspended.

Monetary expansion was associated with an unbridled fall in values and hyper-inflation. Influenced in their actions by their memories, those who held the levers of power hesitated. Before taking action they waited for confirmation that devaluation would not be the precursor of hyper-inflation.

This hesitation had two implications. First since the players did not take advantage of their new-found freedom. The fall in exchange rates gave a boost to exports yet not to internal demand, apart from in those countries where there had also been a build up of internal credit.

The second implication of this hesitation of reflation was that devaluation impoverished others. The devaluation of currencies mainly worked by changing the relative price of imports and exports. Devaluation forced up the price of goods imported, stifling internal demand for merchandise produced by other countries. This made exports from those countries that had devalued more competitive. In 1937, the level of European production was at last higher than in 1929. In America the level in 1937 had not reached that of 1929.

Observers, shocked by the cost of financial instability, quickly set themselves to transforming national and international financial institutions to prevent a repeat of these catastrophic events. To discourage excessive stock market speculation, stricter rules were enforced which limited the volatility of the financial markets. The transformation of the international monetary and financial system was achieved. The international monetary system was reconstructed following the guidelines of the Bretton Woods agreement. The International Monetary Fund was created to act as lender of last resort and to facilitate cooperation between member states. A degree of flexibility in exchange rates became part and parcel of the Bretton Woods system. Countries were allowed to devalue their currency, when forced to choose between maintaining existing parity and full employment.

These innovations were in response to problems revealed by the inter-war crisis of the financial system. Observers, startled by financial instability and its impact on the macroeconomic crisis of the 20's and 30's, congratulated themselves over these new arrangements which seemed to provide for increased stability on two counts.

Yet today we must also judge how far these post-war reforms have been adhered to. The protection represented by the separation of deposit and commercial banks has been abandoned in many countries. Deposit guarantees are under threat in the United States due to banks having difficulties. The World Bank does not have sufficient funds to get rid of the developing nations' debts.

The EMS (European Monetary System) often strays from the system of parity, which is similar to the gold standard. The world seems to be returning to institutions that are closer to those that followed the First World War than those that followed the Second. This raises the question whether the lessons of the inter-war period have been forgotten.

The Dematerialization of Money: Facts and Consequences

Christian de Boissieu

The aim of this article is to put forward a few ideas on the theme of the dematerialization of money. When dealing with this theme one needs to start from a historical comparison. In France at the beginning of the century the majority of monetary instruments were either metal or fiduciary in the form of coins or notes. This characteristic was suited to an economy that was still mainly agricultural. Today metallic currency represents a small percentage of the monetary mass in circulation; banknotes are still around, but their role is less and less important. In every country, be they developed or developing, the role of banknotes is decreasing on the whole as a means of payment.

Money, initially in the form of merchandise (cf. the gold standard, the silver standard or bi-metallic systems which operated in some countries in the nineteenth century) then became fiduciary principally with the growth of banknotes (end of the nineteenth and the beginning of the twentieth century). The transfer of banknotes has been progressively replaced over the twentieth century and in particular since the Second World War by the accountants pen, in other words payments increasingly entail what could be called "universal accounting": the transfer of payment leading to entries into accounts. In recent years with what is called electronic money (or the electronic monetary flow) entries have become computerized and rely on telematics.

Two aspects of this dematerialization will be looked at. First we need to make an inventory of fixtures and prospects for the dematerialization of money. This will be followed by raising a few of the implications of its dematerialization.

The Inventory of Fixtures and Prospects for the Dematerialization of Money

Dematerialization is a general phenomenon which takes place with varying speed according to the country concerned. Yet is a tendency in all the different countries towards electronic money which is increasing with competition. Hence the financial liberalization and competitiveness of Europe with the construction of the common internal market aligns countries that are relatively unsophisticated in this field with those so-called advanced ones, since they wish to maintain the competitiveness of their banking and financial systems and their capital markets.

The phenomenon where the pen of the accountant is replaced by the use of the information keyboard and electronics has many forms that in one way or another concern the relationship between money and information.

Electronic money also involves cards (credit cards that allows for later payment, cash cards that instantly debit, chip cards thought of by a French inventor which contain a lot of information, etc.) automatic cash dispensers (ACD) and automatic bank counters (ABC), the phenomenon of home banking which allows for decentralizing payments and make payments from a distance (telephone payment), etc.

The flow of money through electronics is increasing at a varying pace in different countries. Even when looking at the ODEC countries, these are wide variations. In a sense, France is felt to have a technological advance in the field of electronic money. It is one of the areas where French technology is certainly better than its main partners and especially Germany. Today Germany is clearly behind in the use of cards, even though it is developing quite quickly there. Thus, in 1989, there were 9,300 ACD's and ABC's per 100,000 inhabitants in Germany, as opposed to 13,000 in France. To be behind is an observation but it is not necessarily a handicap. It is useful to gain from the experiments of others. We should not start with the idea that being behind is always bad and that being ahead is always good.

In France the micro chip card was widespread by 1992. The 20 million carriers of cards in France—those with at least one card—have a micro chip card.

Another example of how technologically advanced the French are is provided by the density of the minitel network which is the sector of home banking and telephone buying. Today in France there are about 5 million minitels. The fact that the minitel network is relatively well developed in France is at the same time both an advantage from a technological point of view and maybe a threat in terms of competition. This last point was often underlined in relation to the implications of European integration. It will be easy enough for foreign banks to use the opportunity of the minitel to sell financial products in France without having to set up there, as a free service. The density of the minitel network is generally an advantage in the sense that it means cheaper costs, especially sales costs, and to improve payment technology, yet in another sense it might increase the competition of foreign banks in the internal French market.

Another characteristic of the French payment system is the connection that exists between banks. Thanks to this, the various banking chains, even though they are competitors, have had the sense to find areas of cooperation, each in line with the principle of mutual recognition, formalized by the creation of an economic interest group (EIG), each accepting the cards issued by other chains. The plethora of credit cards in the United States is in part a result of the absence of banking interface, other motives of course also influencing this, such as cards being a sign of class. The interface of its banks is no doubt a trump card in terms of European competition.

In terms of new technologies applied to the running of the stock markets France is steadily catching up with the Anglo-Saxon world (cf. the system of title payment-delivery).

In comparison with some other countries—for example lets continue with Germany which is invariably our touchstone, in a way our obsession—we see that in terms of payment technology and electronic money there are quite wide differences today between France and Germany. In Germany, the majority of payments are made by transfer which also exists in France but has been gradually replaced by more modern forms of settling a bill. In Germany credit cards are relatively undeveloped in comparison to what exists in France.

It is clear that the present differences between France and Germany will continue to disappear as a consequence of the integration of Europe. Germany will be forced rapidly to develop its electronic money and to align itself on the French system as regards payment technology.

The phenomenon of dematerialization of money is not only general, but it is irreversible. In other words, a return of money-merchandise is now very improbable, even though in the economic debate, on an international level, a return to the gold standard or a raw materials standard is sometimes raised. For various reasons these suggestions are hardly credible. In the former USSR, proposals aimed at valuing the ruble against the gold stocks did not last long.

Even with the ex-USSR which has to implement a difficult transition and ensure its credibility, there is no question of its having to return to a currency-merchandise.

What can we expect in the area of further developments of the dematerialization of money? There are still to come some potential advances with the introduction of new technology in paying. There is no reason to expect a halt in the electronic phenomenon of the monetary flow. One should expect the continued dematerialization of the cheque. Cheques represent a large proportion of payments in a country such as France, yet they still involve material transfers, with delays between emission and debiting of the account. One can expect a system of "cheque images" (dematerialized cheques). In this system a cheque received by a shop-keeper would not be transferred from the shop-keeper to other actors (the bank, etc.); all that would happen would be that the image is transmitted, in other words the information that is on the cheque would be sent. The dematerialization of cheques already exists in some countries, for instance Belgium. In France there is a slight delay in the setting up of this system. Those involved are not all ready to take part. For instance, the banks tend now to be slowing the pace of change, since a part of their profits come precisely from the fact that there is a material transfer of cheques and the time-gap between the moment when the cheque is signed and the time that the account is credited or debited. A proportion of French banks rely on the existence of this delay to remain profitable. It is therefore necessary to compensate for the knock-on effects of the setting up of the cheque image system through an unavoidable charge which will be tricky to work out for banking services.

THE CONSEQUENCES OF THE DEMATERIALIZATION OF MONEY

We need to look at some of the consequences of the dematerialization of money, raising no doubt more questions than real answers. In terms of the socio-economic consequences of electronic money, there have been very few studies made or just monographs dealing with a part of the French economy and one would be loath to generalize.

A first question would be on the implications of electronic money on what we might term individual freedom. This is a massive philosophical and economic question that cannot easily be answered.

Electronic money produced both time and space. It makes space because it multiplies the ubiquitous nature of money. Access to payment cards (credit or cash cards) were until very recently an outward sign of wealth or social status. With its spread this value has gradually disappeared. Yet payment cards increases, for everyone who uses one, the freedom to come and go as they please. Electronic money has a hand in the general phenomenon of globalization of economies and trade.

It also produced time through two aspects that are fairly contrasting: on the one hand, electronic money makes use of operations which take place in real time, in other words there is no longer a lapse of time between the moment that an order is given and the moment that it is acted upon. Without going into the economic arguments the system of transfer days would have disappeared for purely technical reasons. This is the success of real time in the field of payment. Yet electronic money also produces time in another sense. It in fact makes time due to the system of what are called credit cards (which are in fact delayed debit cards). The credit card is an instrument that in the short term loosens financial constraints. It is well understood that this is one of the main reasons for its success.

A further question needs to be addressed: what are the consequences of an electronic monetary system on the behavior of the individual? On this broad question here is an initial observation: it is believed—although very hard to prove—that the dematerialization of money changes what psychoanalysts refer to as the relationship between the individual and money. Electronic money in a certain way removes what would be termed the value of objects. Some sociologists believe that electronic money helps some individuals to free themselves from what they call the "money complex," or, at least, to change their relationship to money in comparison with an economy in which there still exists commodity money or one where most operations are carried out in banknotes.

A second aspect of the same question needs to be tackled. What are the consequences of electronic money on the consumption patterns of the individual? Credit cards are a phenomenon which might lead to an increase in consumption, precisely because of the loosening of financial constraints which was mentioned previously. Even so, although it is a generally accepted view, one must not exaggerate the importance of this phenomenon. In France, over the last twenty years, the rate of saving of an average household has tended to go down, at least until 1989-1990. The phenomenon of electronization of monetary exchanges played a minor role in this decline in the rate of saving of couples in a country such as France.

A further aspect needs to be taken into consideration: what are the consequences of electronic money on the ways that economic agents—businesses as well as individuals—manage their cash-flow and wealth? Here one can reply confidently that electronic money has forced households and businesses to manage their cash-flow better. There has therefore been a rationalization of the way economic agents behave in relation to money and wealth. Reducing the cost of unitary transactions, the electronization of monetary flow encourages the mobility of financial capital from on sector of the economy to another, from one country to another, etc., yet at the same time undermining the differences between money and other financial elements; therefore at the same time also the concrete definition of the different aggregates of money. Money has always been hard to grasp conceptually and define in an empirical way. With the process of dematerialization, it is even more so.

Further implications concern the relationship between the banks and their clients. On this question there are also various sub-plots that might be raised. On the one hand, electronic money in some ways increases the role of the bank by making it a technological pole of attraction. On the other, it can also reduce it, since due to electronic money and what is known as the exchange of computer information, businesses can increasingly carry out their own operations without recourse to the banking system. A flow of compensating operations (netting) between the businesses takes place. Banks are therefore experiencing a general reduction of their intermediate role because of technology. There is the risk of banks being by-passed due to new electronic methods which allow businesses and individuals to organise themselves without having to rely on the banking system. This technological side-stepping adds itself to the financial side-stepping which almost everywhere has non-financial agents on the levers of capital markets and direct financing procedures.

An important challenge faces the banks: as a result of the fact that electronic money tends to distance the client from the counter, or again to the extent that physical contact between the bank and their clients is tending to go down, how can they try to restore contact with their clients bearing in mind the unavoidable growth of electronic money? The strategy of the banks in the 1990's, in France as well as abroad, needs to try and answer this question.

A further major question concerning the implications of electronic money revolves around the organisation of exchanges in an economy. To what extent does the growth of electronic money change the network of exchanges in an economy? Without a doubt electronic money allows for the decentralization of exchanges and payments. Everyone can change into a small bank in their own home. There is an unstoppable tendency to decentralization, which would lead one to think that there might be an organisational system set up in the form of a "net," in other words without a centre and without a real centralisation of information. In fact the increasing decentralization that electronic money allows would not be viable or acceptable if it were not accompanied at the same time by a certain centralization of information and process of compensation of payments (clearing) which would be the counter-balance of the decentralization of payments. The procedure of compensation no doubt has a bright future taking into account the increase of decentralization of payments. Behind the opposition between organising a (decentralised) "network" and a (centralised) "web" floats the crucial need for the management of systemic (or global) risks. It is *a priori* easier to limit the financial risks, when they are local, in a decentralised scheme and so avoid the risk of them becoming systemic, even though this advantage is matched by the potential inconvenience that dispersal of information involves. Whatever the case, even in a "net" organisation finance remains global and the phenomena of interconnection needs, on the part of central banks and other monetary and banking authorities appropriate means to contain the systemic risks.

TOMORROW'S MONEY

Jacques Lesourne

Each field of academic study has its own perspective of money. What I would like to do comes both from economics and the study of the uses that society makes of scarce resources with multiple uses and from the art of prospective which ponders on the future and defines possibilities thrown up by chance, human will and necessity.

Yet such a project immediately comes across a difficulty: money is not an invention of economists. This everyday expression contains three specific notions for the economist:

- **currency,** which is used at the same time as an intermediary for exchanges, a standard of value at the present time and over the longer period, a means of accumulating value over time;
- **revenue**, which measures what households have over a period of time to cover their consumption and allow for savings and which nominally or in reality, primarily or at a secondary level is a way to gauge the standard of living yet not the quality of life;
- **wealth**, of the individual or the group, which is equal to the value of the stock of goods possessed by a household, a business or a public company.

Thus we have to keep each of these notions in mind successively to formulate a prospective idea. Such an apportionment presupposes *a contrario* that we identify initially the main tendencies that will influence our thinking.

The first of these main tendencies concerns obviously *demographics*. How can one forget that the world population will continue to grow rapidly to reach 8 billion in 2025 despite the steady slow-down of the annual growth rate. With a surplus that will mainly be in the third world whereas the population of the developed world will stagnate. The demographic increase will be accompanied by dense migrations: inside the countries, from the countryside to the towns, between countries, developing regions to the industrialized zones. Logically a prospective of money should concentrate on the relations to money of the 6-7 billion people on very low incomes who in 35 years time will form the majority of humanity.

The change in man's relation with the ecosystem forms the second main tendency. Whether it involves the reduction of carbon gas emissions, protection of the ozone layer, maintenance of biodiversity or the protection of the environment in some regions of the planet (acid rain and land-locked seas), we will probably feel the effects of setting out obligatory international norms or the appearance of specific taxes. This is the dawn of a whole area of the economic landscape which is not commercial.

We also have to mention the globalization of economies which has continued to increase since the Second World War and which seems unstoppable despite the resurgence of nationalism. It affects the markets, trade markets, work markets, service markets—above all financial—economic factors which are becoming increasingly transnational and finally the states. The latter find themselves more and more in a situation of co-sovereignty (this will be the case at the end of the century for the monetary policy of the European nations that have joined the EMU). They also offer public services which large businesses look at when deciding to relocate parts of their organisation. Without a doubt the future of money will be profoundly influenced in the following decades by the globalization of economic phenomena.

Finally the last main tendency that I wanted to raise was the growing place of *information technology*. Of course the process has continued over the last forty years but it is far from being over. By giving humanity the intellectual instrument of computer programs and databases, by allowing at the same time the transmission of huge amounts of information and communication in an instant to people spread out across the globe, computers and telecommunications contribute to the development of an "immaterial" activity which will henceforth underpin every material production in society. Currency, revenue and wealth will seriously be affected.

These brief pointers to the general prospective show how much the idea of money is linked to all the social and economic evolutions that man will experience.

MONEY AND ITS EVOLUTION

In their first lesson on money, students of economics learn that it has four functions and first of all it is an *intermediary of exchange*. In this sense the tendency which stretches back to the dawn of history is clearly unambiguous: from heads of cattle to bits of metal, from metal coins to banknotes, from cheques to magnetic cards, money has progressively become immaterial. Undoubtedly with the explosion of new information technologies this dematerialization will continue apace and will permeate growing layers of the world's population. Even so, there will coexist for a long time on the planet groups of people living in self-sufficiency and barter and networks of individuals using only "electronic currency."

As for the role of money as a standard it has been brutally reaffirmed with the collapse of the command economies of eastern Europe. In fact it was their lack of efficiency due mainly to the lack of a pricing system able to force the economic players to adapt to the situation of offer and demand, which convinced Gorbachev and his advisers to implement *perestroika*. In the same way the IMF and the World Bank in the last few years have continued to warn many third world countries of the need for real prices, a reality of pricing which does not exclude a parallel policy of redistribution of income and wealth. Unfortunately prices exist that in the world economy at the moment have become remote from their value as a balancing mechanism and undermine the choices of economic agents: interest rates. Hence the importance of international macroeconomic management to ensure the balance of payments of the largest industrialised countries. One thing is sure: the central role of price in the direction of the structure of world production will continue over the next quarter of a century. This proposition is not in contradiction to the other prognoses that will elaborated later.

A third function of money is to enable an *accumulation of values over time* in the form of an asset that can be liquid, in other words can be used at any time without delay or cost for the transaction. As a compensation, traditionally this asset did not carry any interest. There resulted a clear difference between money and other assets that could be liquidated with more difficulty and gave interest. Yet this difference has been eroded during the 1970's. Today we can see a variety of assets that have different liquidity and interest rates. Economists have also been forced to introduce several concepts of monetary mass M1, M2, M3, and so forth. As for finance ministers they have had to forget about regulating the monetary markets since the economic system was escaping from their restrictions by developing the use of unregulated assets. Hence the general use of interest rates by a central bank as the variant of control. Yet in an open economy this variation also has an effect on exchange rates and its use is therefore very much dictated by international circumstances.

Then finally the last function of money is that of standard of value over time. In fact, a 100 franc note allows one at any time—as long as it is still in circulation—to acquire 100 francs of goods or services. Yet every consumer is well aware that money fulfills very badly this criterion because of inflation. Inflation, whose rate varies between a few points and a few hundred percent, without forgetting the case of hyper-inflation where the rate is even higher and leads to the collapse of the country's monetary system. At the moment there are two areas of the world that are being eaten away by high inflation: parts of Latin America and some countries in central and eastern Europe. Nobody can rule out the possibility of hyper-inflation in Russia similar to that of Germany at the start of the 1920's. Among the consequences of inflation two need to be emphasized:

- the gap between the nominal and real interest rates that can ruin the borrower or the lender in contracts with fixed interest rates when the market misjudges price rises;
- the resulting appearance of economic agents who gain from it and therefore try and keep it going.

What lessons for the future does this short study suggest? I propose three:

1) Money will continue to become dematerialized and the difference between it and other assets will be reduced. Henceforth interest rates will be the main mechanism of monetary policy.
2) Tomorrow as in the past, countries struck by economic, social or political crisis might be struck by inflation that might go out of control.
3) A system of prices, reflecting more or less accurately the relative scarcity of various resources on a world level will continue to operate over the next few decades and to model production, with all countries becoming more engaged in a free market economy whatever the complexion of their government.

The role of prices will be looked at in terms of income.

THE DILEMMA OF INCOME

In every society, the income of a household derives from two often contradictory logics:

- on the one hand, payment of services made to the collectivity (in this perspective a monthly salary is a price like any other);
- on the other, it is a condition of the standard of living of a family and the political powers in the name of equity can not ignore its distribution.

It is useful to remember these two approaches. For the first it is better to speak of *labour costs* rather than salary. What is novel is the steady growth, through international trade, of a world labour market in which offer and demand of various natures compete. Yet the entry on this market of a growing proportion of the adult population—generally unskilled—in the third world translates itself in a relative increase of highly skilled offers of work and relative growth of demands for unskilled jobs. Hence an increase in the labour costs of highly skilled individuals rather than unskilled, even more exaggerated due to computerization and automation. This means in plain speaking that if there was no redistribution the inequality of the distribution of incomes would increase in European countries. The existence of a minimum wage has slowed this down, but in maintaining the labour cost of unskilled individuals above the level of equilibrium it has produced a rate of unemployment that is long-term. This unemployment that economists refer to as "classic" needs to be distinguished from the Keynesian sort which is a product of lack of demand. How can we fight against it? In the long-term by improving the skills of the least skilled workers. In the short-term, by lowering the cost of their labour in the workplace, or topping up their primary income with income support.

Let us remember that governments will no longer be able to modify labour costs on the national market, since the hierarchy of costs will mainly be controlled by the world market.

Unemployment can always be analyzed in terms of classic unemployment, Keynesian or frictional. Some predict that unemployment will increase as a consequence of the wish of individuals to accept lower wages and to consume less. Yet how can they not appreciate that, if this is the case, there will also be a decline in the demand for work (individuals wishing to lower the time spent working) and a lessening of offer of work (businesses facing up to the fact that demand for their products goes down); a balance of the labour market would be reached a lower level of jobs. False logic continues to thrive.

Neither should we believe that the problem of labour costs concerns only the developed world. In some regions of the third world—in sub-Sahara Africa especially—the minimum salary of the urban sector are way above their real value, even though they might appear to us to be very low. One need only look at the level of pay of small farmers and the parallel market. This distortion contributes to under-employment which is often seen in developing nations.

Income, as an indicator of the standard of living highlights two main problems.

Even if it were correctly measured bearing in mind consumption, what is its relationship with the quality of life. It is good taste in some sectors of public opinion of countries with a good standard of living to deny any correlation, yet the behavior of the majority of the population of those countries—salary demands above all—show how wide off the mark this judgment is. As for the third world masses, they undoubtedly aspire to a rise in their income. I would suggest a double prognosis: 1) in those countries with a high standard of living, monetary income and quality of life will increasingly diverge and individual demand will in the future be more concerned on qualitative aspects of their existence; 2)in countries with a low standard of living, on the contrary, the best inspired governments will attempt to attain at the same time a rapid development and an improvement of the quality of life for the most impoverished.

Whether it is or not an essential element in the quality of life, income also poses the problem of distribution or rather its redistribution.

Redistribution among the members of the same generation at the heart of a national society. Taxes and public services have traditionally been the tools used to effect this redistribution. Yet it encounters two difficulties at the present time: the emergence in the commercial sector of undesirable consequences due to high obligatory contributions and the growing inability of the welfare state to manage effectively this redistribution. Also, with the current liberal wave, will democratic societies continue to look for political means for a moderate and effective redistribution?

Redistribution also between successive generations. This is the usual role of investment. Yet two questions are raised about this: will the rate of interest which results from offer and demand for capital by operators now produce the necessary balance of funds that humanity will need in the future? Should actualization be allowed at the risk of depriving future generations of essential resources? In other words, should not humanity preserve the wealth of future generations? Posed in these terms the proposal carries a positive response yet it hides some formidable variants: the notion of resources depends on the epoch, technical progress makes certain resources useless and creates others and engenders new needs.

The balance of generations leads us logically to the last theme that I suggested, that of wealth. Yet prior to examining it, I would like to voice some of the beliefs that I have built up after years of prospective studies:

- the world's income per capita will continue to rise over the next decades, growth being unhindered by physical limits;
- even so, humanity needs increasingly to worry about protecting the ecosystem and consequently control this growth;
- the lifting of trade barriers will stop the rate of growth of developed countries continuing to be visibly different;
- the average growth of third world nations will be higher than that of developed nations, yet this will not result in a closing of the gap between the incomes of the richest and the poorest;
- in the long-term the need for redistribution will become more pressing, above all in relation to the areas of the globe that are least developed.

THE DIVERSITY OF WEALTH

In simple terms, "to have money" raises not only the possible level of monthly expenditure, but the amount of wealth available, wealth that might have many forms, from money to bonds to shares, land or petrol deposits, real estate to machines, copyright to computers.

Yet the *paradox of this wealth,* which for the man of the street seems to have an innate price, since it is made up of actual goods, is that it only has a value in terms of future use that it might be put to for its owners. The most modern steel plant, whatever the cost of building, ceases to have a value if the state of the market in the future does not allow it to sell its production at a price that covers its running costs. Every day technical progress undermines elements of wealth. A difficult phenomenon to understand when the workers discover that the machines they are working have to go to the breakers, even though they are in perfect working order. This paradox has a corollary: the value of wealth depends on the future expectations of those in control of an economy. In other words the value of a tangible stock of goods is conditioned by something which is delicate to appreciate in a society, the projection of the future. Previously turned to the past, since the future reflected the past, wealth finds its significance in the future, in a world in which economic structures are permanently evolving.

To attempt a real analysis of the prospective of wealth would lead us too far, yet three aspects of such an analysis must be mentioned.

We are seeing a *progressive dematerialization of wealth.* This is the reverse side of the increasing weight of immaterial investment, research, education, organisation, programming, advertising, in every area of the production of gross fixed capital. In a country such as France, immaterial investment already represents a quarter of the total investment and this percentage is increasing rapidly. A business who launches a hostile take-over on a competitor is not doing it to get its machines. It is much more interested in its technology, the quality of its personnel, the stage of research and the volume of its markets.

We can also see that wealth cannot be reduced to the goods that will be commercialized, or in other words sold at a certain price. Alongside the commercial wealth, there exists a *non-commercial wealth*: so an arms system for national defense has a value if it is up-to-date and if it is in response to a plausible threat, yet its use cannot be judged by its price in the market. At most we can arrive at an implicit indirect estimate by studying the judgment made by society of its usefulness and other commercial imperatives. What is the importance of commercial wealth in relation to non commercial wealth? This is a difficult question since the limits of commercial and non-commercial are permanently changing.

Finally, the last major component of a prospective on wealth: how will the *distribution of wealth* between households, private concerns and public services evolve? How should we view the concept of commonwealth of humanity, a concept that not only encapsulates natural resources but the genetic stock of species, unalterable facts of climate, the totality of spoken and written languages, the totality of human knowledge? How should we manage this common wealth? There is no question of being able to keep it in its present form, since the everyday actions of people enriches it as well as destroys it, yet in the end it will be necessary to decide on the future, in other words the balance of creation and destruction, bearing in mind the idea that we hold of the desires of future generations.

Should we be surprised? When talking about money we have rediscovered all the major themes of contemporary perspectives and from this study has emerged what could be called *an ethic of balance*, a moral of compromise that orders man to judge, in all its dimensions, the consequences of decisions that he might take and then weigh these evaluations. Some are financial other are not. Money is essential as a gauge of things but it is not the measure of everything. It will be the same tomorrow as it is today.

Law and Money

Does Everything have a Price?

Dany Cohen

The way in which things are couched (especially important for lawyers) is of primal importance: the title here is not *Money and Law*—about which there would be much to comment. Here the given order aims to show, perhaps from a naive reflex and the partiality of a lawyer, that the law was there *first*. The law is consubstantial with the existence of a society: once there is more than one person on a desert island the law is born and the beginnings of a legal system; money in the monetary sense of the term, comes afterwards. I would add that money sometimes loses its authenticity. There exists counterfeit money. I do not believe that a counterfeit law exists.

Money should here be understood in its monetary sense, yet perhaps we might go further and enlarge it to its pecuniary, economic value of what lawyers term as goods.

It is a commonplace to say that money is everywhere, and the law is happy where it can of course channel it. They live in close proximity—and this expression is intended to show that between money and the law there exists the kind of complicity which, as can be observed with many couples, goes hand in hand with partial rejection. Of course, the law gives money a role and perhaps a large role, yet here again words are of importance. When the law presumes to give money a role, or in other words organize the relationship with money within society, it attempts, as a system, to imprint its mark on the socio-economic life; it pretends to be the organizer of all monetary flow which not only spills a little but largely runs out of control. Of course, we can recall obvious examples such as exchange controls which showed that there were judicial rules. Even the freedom of commercial and monetary transactions are in themselves a phenomenon of legal organisation precisely since this freedom is granted, allowed for by the rule of law, which feeds the idea, at least in part illusory, that exchanging of money takes place under its control. No doubt this is the result of dialectics, of an image of domination, of organization, that legal science and practice portray themselves, uncomfortably at times, as the protector of money and in turn of those who possess it. It has been often said that the French civil code, which is a model in judicial terms, and was often copied abroad, was a code for property owners. This is proven by the pride of place given to pecuniary aspects in this thick tome.

This body of evidence however allows for shady areas to remain. One is initially struck by the fact that money is present in legal areas where one would expect it to be, but also in those where one would not, while on the contrary it is absent from some in which we would expect it. Finally, there are some areas where money is present, however discretely, where it enters through the back door, apologetically.

Taken as a broad sketch, there are first of all two basic situations:

- one that is narrow yet firm, easy to observe, where money is forbidden, excluded from our judicial system and others;
- another where it is the opposite, and which means that money is lord and master.

Alongside these basic positions (perhaps in between?) there has developed a third category, possibly the most subtle, most interesting, where money is a substitute or a palliative.

Let us start at the beginning: there are situation where money is excluded, which is to say that there are things that are "priceless." Here again, the ambiguity of the term is important. To have no price signifies precisely that it has one but it is impossible to calculate. Something that is priceless is precisely what is worth the most in our ladder of values. This is not surprising in itself. Yet at the heart of the category of things that are priceless one can further distinguish. Hence friendship, which everyone knows cannot be bought, is not only outside monetary relations but also outside the legal domain: there are no legal rules in this field.

Other phenomena that at first glance are foreign to money are on the contrary part of the legal landscape. Our laws speak of things that are "not for sale" pointing out that there are objects which can never be part of a transaction. This notion of things being not for sale is not new. In classical times it was already present: the Romans, a legalistic people, were familiar with things that could not be sold, which were not always the same as our own. For them people could not be sold—yet this was for freemen since those who were not could be sold. The principle was basically the same as now; only its applications differed.

We say now that a human being cannot be sold—not a living being since plants and animals can be bought and sold.

Freedom also at present cannot be sold, which shows a development from only the 19th Century when debtors could be imprisoned, which means that the freedom of an individual might be worth less than a monetary debt. In this way, it could be said that money's importance has declined in the legal hierarchy of values of our civilisation. A human being, living or dead, nor his freedom—in the most basis sense of the word—can not be the subject of a financial transaction.

Yet one hesitates before taking a further step and state that the body cannot be sold. Of course, a contract of prostitution is meaningless, although this does not prevent it existing. What then, in front of this tangible reality, does a meaningless contract mean? Simply a contract in which there is no recourse to law: the client who has paid the prostitute can always later try and complain to a court, if services have been withheld; evidently there would be no legal redress.

The meaningless of contracts passed with surrogate mothers has emerged more recently. God alone knows how worked up people got over this "vacuum of law," how it was stated that there were no guidelines, that the legal systems were powerless in front of such unexpected situations and technological progress. It is not clear whether things are so novel and there is no legal vacuum. Guidelines do exist, as laid down by the High Court and operating, since they derive from the great principles of our laws: the contract of surrogate mothers is null and void. I would personally agree with this solution, bearing in mind that other people disagree. I still believe that it is just and right that a woman's womb cannot be rented out. I do not deny that people do it in the same way that there are motorists who go through a red light.

To suggest, however, that this is a new problem, that has never been thought about, is to be blinded by the technological feat. Do people really have to be conscious of the reality, technologically speaking, to consider and decide on what might happen, dialectically and even philosophically? The question is really to whom should the child belong when it is conceived and carried in unusual circumstances; initially considered in classical times with the children of slaves when a woman slave, who was an object, was lent by her master to someone else, and gave birth to a child. To whom did the child belong? it was then asked. This parallel which Professor Francois Terré makes is not so simple, to the extent that the contracts for surrogacy do not always operate in circumstances where there is absolute gift or for people of similar socio-economic background, but even where it is slightly different there is still a similarity which means that the thoughts of the Roman lawyers cannot be ignored.

The recent position of the High Court on this question shows that sometimes the rights of money are restricted—more or less—a resistance to the idea that it is right to be always a "realistic" and that judicial rulings should be no more than a mirror of the reality, according to strictly prosaic concepts, devoid of morality.

Let us be grateful that human organs and blood also can not be sold.

Whereas money is absolutely excluded by law from these narrow areas of activity, there are a great many other fields where money is not allowed, but where under pressure it does operate. Here I have in mind our civil liberties, which are meant to have such a value that we cannot give them up and they cannot be paid for. There are many examples, among which sacking is the most striking. An employer is always free to make an employee redundant and one could, simplifying it, say that the legal rules are mainly there to establish the method rather than altering that freedom. Let us now imagine that an employer sacks an employee unlawfully. Everybody knows that if this is brought in front of a court and the illegality is proven then the employer will normally be found against but will not be forced to take the employee back, only to pay a fine. Thus what initially was unnegotiable becomes so, with a few exceptions. For example, since September 26,1990, the High Court decided that if an employer sacks an employee for striking, he cannot change this irregular sacking by means of a straightforward payment. Since the right to strike is a civil freedom the employer should not be able, according to the Court, estimate in terms of money in advance the unlawful action that he commits, and in this case, although this is an exception, it forced the reinstatement of the worker rather than accept payment. The reality is plainly more down to earth, since most of the strikers are not naive enough to hope to be taken back on by the company.

There is also the other extreme where money is king. The dominant, protean rights of business, rights of businessmen in the broadest sense of the term, developed to control economic exchanges are often cited. They are many-faceted rights, amongst which of course fiscal rights. Businesses and managers are constantly worrying about how much tax they have to pay. The reverse side of fiscal law is evident: where many see only an enormous needle meant to pump the economic players there is also an extraordinarily complex network of interconnected mechanism which offer a string of fiscal benefits. The latter are often perceived in a strange way by the public, who see them almost as a way of avoiding the law, as though there should be no benefits, as though economic policy was not implemented through using monetary devices and especially varying taxes and consequently related benefits.

Yet to speak of the right of money means going far beyond the rights of business, since the right of work or even civil law are linked to this side of our commercial economy. Even though civil law is not specifically about economic relations everything has its price. All the things that surround us could have a price tag. These are uncontrolled or almost all. If we sell at too high a price there is almost never any problem. If we sell too low there might in certain circumstances be a problem—yet not in every case—which shows clearly that the judicial rules share a relationship with relative value, in certain rare problems, of the economic value of some things, in conclusion that the law interferes in judging the value of things. Thus the contract of sale in which the price is not declared would be null and void whatever other conditions were to apply. The contract is null and void under the same circumstances because there is no price. This would seem obvious yet this system is not universal.

Let us go deeper. Money is in many cases interwoven with the rule of law in situations where theoretically it should not have a role. Taking one example, how many Personnel Managers or employers have explained that they want to sack such and such an employee, yet because of the work code, they cannot act just as they please. They look at their calculator, work out the risk, decide on the costs—a typical case where the law is defeated by money, where a business knows it cannot proceed the way it would want, yet decides to flout this, to take a calculated risk after anticipating the possible costs of breaking this judicial rule.

We encounter a much more serious problem with what is known in legal terminology as obligation. Although it is a technical term the concept is no less important for what we are looking at here: a teacher who has to take a class has an obligation. Yet if he shirks, how can he be forced? Of course, this is a caricature although the principle remains true whether we nuance it or not. Above all, we see that the situation might arise in very different circumstances. Thus the Civil Code states in article 1142 that all obligations are to be resolved through paying damages, which is obvious but also shows impotence: when it is impossible to force someone to do something that he had agreed to do, there only remains the possibility of compensation. An idea based on realism(what else can one do?) sometimes throws up the possibility of distortion, so that the decision to respect or flout an obligation comes from a monetary calculation which shows that the sanctions of the rule of law are at least as important as the rule itself and in so many circumstances an economic calculation might lead to avoiding obligations since the creditor of the obligation would not be able to enforce it. The economic calculation is encouraged in France by what I am tempted to call the stinginess of the courts in contrast to the generous compensations granted in the States. This money given in repayment closes the question of a stalemate.

This observation leads us to a third series of situations, possibly the most unusual, the most subtle, where money serves as a replacement. It comes in through a side-entrance, it nothing more than a last resort and soon becomes all-important in a field where normally it should not be present. It is an intruder. Professor Cottereau would explain how this system operates which leads to the victim being compensated for a certain amount of events with damages.

The judicial structure of these situations is unchanged although their actual diversity is infinite. There is private life, the protection of the privacy of individuals and their image. I have in mind the case of the wife of a colleague who was photographed while out shopping in a supermarket accompanied by her children at the end of the summer holidays. The photo appeared, without the consent of the subject, on the front page of a newspaper illustrating the preparations for the return to school. There was a court case, and the paper was forced to pay compensation: everyone has the right over their own picture. Yet what could be done once the offense had taken place, when the photo had already appeared, once the injury to your privacy had occurred? It cannot be blotted out, there is nothing else than pay compensation, or there is no redress. Money here plays the dual role of redresser—when the offense has been committed—and threat intended to dissuade, if possible, those inclined to infringe on the privacy of others.

The same applies to the case for individual freedom. Someone suspected of having committed a crime might be imprisoned and it later turns out that the person is innocent. Even a few years ago the victim would only have got a few words of apology. These are now followed by compensation, which seems only fair. Even so, I should draw your attention to the fact that the sums involved are quite small in such circumstances, so the economic incentive favours not being imprisoned.

There remains only the area of love and more especially divorce. In divorce proceedings, the frequency of conflict over the question of money shows indirectly but clearly that this is a derivative, that the protagonists are fighting at least in part over things that have nothing to do with money, which is but a substitute, meant to hide other things, to give a material delineation—more acceptable—to things that have nothing to do with it. This kind of materialization is often useful.

There is finally what is called the price of suffering, the price of life and the price of tears. This morning we talked about accidents and illness. In the same perspective, one can cite a well known judgment by the State Council, delivered in 1968, in a case where a young woman underwent surgery during which a medical error occurred, which resulted in the victim being unable to have sexual relations without having acute pain. The State Council judged that she had suffered injury to the tune of 20,000 francs (in 1968). Is it surprising that in this most intimate of areas there is a price? One could be struck by the sum—bearing testimony of the modest importance granted by the state councillors to certain acts of love—but also by the principle. Should we compensate for this? An answer to this question should not be seen independently from related aspects, for example the "price of life," which is an expression who's significance varies according to its context (a life has no price when it is a question of medical treatment). It has been said that life is priceless in peacetime and above all in a rich society. Are we so certain? To die is clearly not an injury: it has to happen and will. Those that suffer are those left behind and it is in respect to them that the law is in a predicament. In our system of civil responsibility, there are two principles that stipulate that one must repair damage caused and that this reparation should be in kind, or to put it another way it must try to restore things to the state they were in, prior to the injurious event. In the hypotheses that I have just mentioned and obviously in the case of death, it is impossible to restore things to what they were before. This is why they resort to what is called reparation "in its pecuniary equivalent." Horrible expression! Not because it implies that the loss of a loved one has a specific value, but because it presumes that monetary reparations are satisfactory. Until 1962, the State Council mainly stated: it is incalculable. It is so incalculable that you will get nothing. That year they changed their attitude and agreed on estimating what theoretically was incalculable. This is at the heart of the argument: is it right to allocate money in such cases? It was even said that it was shocking that those who remained behind should ask for money! But why are they asking for money? Who can infer that they are exclusively moved by pecuniary motives? How can we judge? It is easy to see such behavior in terms of the need to apportion responsibility for disaster. After a death there is the need to act, to organise the burial and in a way to really mourn. In this way the giving of compensation closes the chapter. In any case, if the money did not go to those survivors who have suffered, then whom would it go to other than the insurance companies who would keep it?

In conclusion, what seems to emerge is that money exposes, in a photographic sense, the situations where the individual and society are equally unable to cope. Once the catastrophe has happened we remain as disarmed as our ancestors would have been over the centuries over events which, with the scientific and technological progress that our civilisation has made, revolt us more and more. Added to which is the fact that our society has become increasingly prosperous. It has the financial means to calm certain situations, yet it is unable to do anything else. It would be naive to believe that what it gives is the price of a life, tears and suffering. The money is nothing more than an admission of impotence, in the final analysis a sign of hopelessness. Feeling powerless, society and the judges are unable to say anything to the victim other than: take it or leave it.

The Relative Nature of the Price of Life

Gilles Cottereau

The price of life is relative. Its relativity is a question that makes us uneasy, at least for us westerners who rather hope that in this area there is a strict equality; perhaps a vertical equality when fundamentally we feel and take for granted the dizzying escalation of expenditure needed to save the life of a person. The one who is dying sees those who love him gathered round his bed saying to you: "His life is priceless. Go on! Spend as much as is needed!" Horizontal equality as well. Yes death strikes us all: this is the human condition. Therefore why distinguish between the dead? The certainty of the event justifies the strictness of the general law: nothing. All individuals will die. Since death is certain, why on earth should death be compensated according to the circumstances of a single life, and the circumstances of a single death? This vertical and horizontal equality is not the answer that organized societies give through their judicial systems. The price of life is considered as relative in time and space. It is be better to die of AIDS following a blood transfusion this year after the law compensating this death has been voted, rather than in the days when there was not recognized responsibility. In short throughout history, in different places, in the various judicial systems of different civilisations, the answer is different. Let us sum this up by giving a historical certainty: one Frank (as Clovis understood the term) was worth two Galls; for the Frankish monarchy a Frank was worth two Galls. Here is a relativity of the price of a life that will shock us now.

The relative value of the price of life could be looked at from various points of view. "Life is not worth living," says the bedridden invalid. In this saying are the words referring to money or to value in itself? No, these words are not linked to money but reveal a further equivalence: "My life is not worth the bother (the price of the bother) of living."

We could also question the relativity of the price of life by looking at an idea of Roger-Pol Droit and by extending the meaning of what we term injury. Now in every judicial system, in an overwhelming way, we compensate only certain types of injury: loss of wealth, what we might hope to earn, and even moral injury, although only within certain judicial systems. There is very little compensation for global social injury. Of course it is only through phenomena such as large scale catastrophes that we are starting to question the very notion of injury. In a sense, it is clear that in this light a child would have a lesser value since it would not have benefited yet from the investment that society puts on each individual; the elderly in this field as in others rejoins childhood; an adult in relation to their place on the ladder of life would therefore have a very different value.

Relative value of the price of life. Perhaps more to the point, or more accurate, if rather sad, one has to admit that one needs to reflect on the price of death, on its compensation (compensation for the loss and for the tears). This compensation is eminently variable depending on the judicial system. The relativity that lies at the heart of a system and which exist—you can see it when discussing with insurance companies—increases whenever an international element is included in the equation.

To understand this we must make a small theoretical detour on one crucial point. Law is a phenomenon that is linked to the state. The state today is a territory, essentially a physical country. It is therefore upon territorial competence that judicial systems have been built up. This is how humanity have organized themselves, or at least this is the system that has succeeded in organizing humanity. It is naturally not the only system imaginable. On might have imagined judicial systems far from being linked to public interest over a territorial area, being born of brotherhood, tribe or ethnicity. So the law might have applied to such and such a group and the relations would not have been international, between different states covering different territories, but rather international because involving different ethnic groups. This is not the case and the territorial system has won. Yet individuals have not stayed put. By moving they have of course made contact with other judicial systems, of necessity they come under the power of different laws. Even within a judicial system, it is reasonable to wonder whether the rules of another state might not apply.

This movement of people unleashes the possibility of variable circumstances. Or else the circumstances needed to bring compensation are wholly present—either in space, the principal actor, the guilty party and the victim—within a judicial order, and there is no need to take into account any international element; or else one of these elements is extraneous to the unity of the state: the principal actor is foreign, people of another nationality die while away from their country, etc. In this situation where there is a foreign element introduced, the other country's rules should be considered. The first case (wholly taking place within the limits of the state) need not be considered. We should look at the case or the circumstance where a foreign element is introduced and a different law to the state's law is taken into account to reach a decision.

All this concerns relations between private individuals. Yet there of course exist circumstances where the party responsible for the loss of life is the state. Here again, if the circumstance solely involves one state alone them we are not interested in the problem. On the contrary if there is a foreign element, in other words for example if the state is responsible for the death of someone who is a foreigner or someone who is not on its territory, then the problem is interesting since an international element has been brought into the question. Here the answer arises out of what is called international public law. Yet we shall see that there are a number of difficulties.

Firstly questions that arise from private contacts between people, what is called private international law. In any given legal system there exists a clear relativity in estimates of the price of the life of an individual. Taking examples of cases that were largely settles in France in 1990 within the court of appeal, I hazard a guess that there are many others. So and so dies. His illegitimate son received 20,000 francs, as moral injury—I am not talking of his rights to the estate which would depend on his wealth, age, etc. In the same court of appeal in the same year, on the death of a woman, a mother who was a widow (so there is no father and the children were orphans) each of the children received due to moral injury for the death of their mother, 30,000 francs. So we have 20,000 in one case and 30,000 in another within the same legal system and in the same year.

This relativity, which exists in the decisions of the judges, becomes even greater if an international element were to be introduced. Without needing to go into detail, one should bear three things in mind. Firstly that international private law, what is known as such, is despite its name, not really international but is the law of the state: each country has its own private international law. Therefore there might be big differences from country to country. Secondly the rule that is invoked will vary depending on the link that exists between the principal and the victim. The same rule will not apply, or rather a rule of the same country, if the link is contractual (if the loss of life is a result of the improper execution of a contract) or if the loss of life is as a result of what is called a felony, in other words a circumstance that does not arise out of a contract.

Finally, the third point: the substantive rule, which will apply, can be fundamentally different. International private law belongs to each state. French international private law will give the ruling on what should be applied if some French people die in a car accident in Spain. There is no guarantee that the same law will apply when Spanish people die in a car accident in France. International conventions do exist, yet there is no *a priori* guarantee that enforces uniformity. Therefore private international law applies different rules according to circumstances. If there is a contract between the principal and the victim, then most systems of private international law, yet not all, would agree that it is contract law that should be used. If there is no contract, if the responsibility is as a result of a felony, it will be the law of the place the felony occurred in that will apply and in some cases the place where the injury took place. This might result in some very complicated circumstances, and attempts to rationalize them have been made. Yet one can see that this idea of a foreign element, combined with the idea of a contract or the absence of one, in a common situation such as a car accident, might result in some extremely complicated circumstances, that could *a priori* be totally different depending on the country. If this has not be harmonized through conventions there would be a very different situation for an accident involving French in Spain if the passenger of a car is carried for free, and for another accident happening to French motorists in Spain when the passenger is carried following a contract. In theory, wherever there is a contractual situation then the laws of contract apply and these people passed their contract in France; where there has been a felony then the law of the land where the felony took place applies, and since the accident happened in Spain, it is the Spanish law that will apply. One can imagine the complications that might result if a French vehicle crashed into a Turkish vehicle in Germany which in turn hit a Swedish vehicle..., if at least a minimum of harmonization had not been introduced. This rationalization obviously has been introduced for car accidents but also for liability for manufactured goods. There a goods that after having been made are sent around the world and in some cases are given under contract and sometimes without. Therefore an attempt has been made to rationalize things.

The laws that apply are not necessarily based on the same rules. This may appear surprising. Let us look at a particular case. In theory German law does not have, or at least does not have in the same way as French law, the notion of moral injury. Therefore, applying French private international law after the death of a French person in Germany, they have to apply German law, it would be impossible for the French judge to give compensation to those who have suffered injury—the family perhaps—and loss because the German law applies. The French judge who was faced with these circumstances felt it was really worrying that compensation for loss or injury of a French person who died in France in similar circumstances to a French person in Germany should be any different. A judge decided, in the name of French public interests, to compensate the injury which is not covered by German law, to restore equality. The High Court decided that this judgment had to be overturned since it would lead to the compensation for loss and injury of Germans in Germany, since their own law do not cover this.

Let us take a concrete example: So and so married with 8 children dies. Financial settlement: for the partner, 26,000 francs for funeral costs, plus—this man made a good living—2,356,000 francs damages, in other terms compensation for the loss of income brought on by his death; for the four sons and four daughters the compensation goes from 96,000 for the oldest who has had the longest support from his parents to 274,000 for the youngest who will suffer most in life from the absence of his father and the material benefits that might have come his way. For loss and suffering for the same family: for the partner 70,000 francs; for the children between 15,000 for those who have had the most to 35,000 for those who had the least in damages. If German law applied then they would have to deduct 70,000, 35,000 and 15,000.

Notwithstanding the slightly technical nature of this problem, these rules of procedure to determine which laws apply do raise ethical questions. Let us write a fable, which it must be said, puts the law in a bad light, yet is useful to understand. Let us imagine an American company that runs, in a poor country, a part of its production system. A catastrophe happens in this country. This raises the question of compensation for this disaster. A large American company producing a dangerous product in a poor country is unbelievable, of course, for Bhopal and Union Carbide is just fiction.... The judge who considers this question—leaving aside the question of who would be judge, whether Indian or American—should they compensate at what I see as a Californian level or should it be Indian. If a Californian type settlement is given, then the Californians who may have been affected by this explosion would see the decision as fair. The Indians who receive this Californian settlement would in their own society brusquely become quasi millionaires (judging from the settlements for loss of life in the American system). In other words, Mister X who dies following an explosion on the site of an American company would be given greater compensation than his next-door neighbour Mister Y who dies after an explosion in an Indian company. Yet if an Indian compensation were given would it not encourage negligence? Why not produce the most dangerous substances in a place where life is cheapest? Here is an ethical problem that can not simply be settled by saying: "Insurance premiums should therefore be raised, including in poor countries, so that the risks covered go much higher" since this would pose an economic problem that is very complicated.

Let us leave these problems of private international law to ponder now those questions that arise from public international law. The actions of a country might bring about the death of people. These actions might be of an illicit or legal sort. Let us examine the case of a state that through an illicit act, something that is not allowed, causes loss of life—obviously in an international context. The individual who is the victim of the situation is unable as an individual to start proceedings against the country. If a private individual wishes to ask for compensation against the French government in a court in their own country they would come across the jurisdictional immunity of other countries and would not be heard. For compensation to occur the problem has to be one of public international law. The transformation of the problem from private takes place through a complicated mechanism—which is best left out—and which is termed diplomatic protection. It is clear that when a country recognizes its own responsibility, or else has it imposed on it (when an international judge, a referee, forces it to accept) compensation is far higher—it is hard to ascertain the real figure for how much a country might pay—much higher than in internal legal settlements.

Here too—we have been asked to be concrete therefore so be it and try and take an example that is familiar to all—in the Rainbow

Warrior affair, the ship that was sunk (negligently) by two secret service officers, there was a person involved. Not only did they sink the boat but they killed Mr. Perrera. The latter was a photographer working for Greenpeace. This photographer who came from Portugal was a Dutch citizen. There was some argument and then France accepted responsibility. If the relatives of Mr. Perrera had wanted to bring a case they could not have won. For the case to become international the Netherlands which was his official country would have had to back it and bring France to trial. While New Zealand was prepared to accuse France for diplomatic reasons which are now well known, the Netherlands were extremely loath to do so. Mr. Perrera would not have managed to get a settlement from the New Zealand courts because jurisdictional immunity applies to country-states. France ultimately accepted responsibility and reached a settlement with the Perrera family. The amount that was given to the Perrera family strikes me as much larger than the sums allocated in internal cases. The French government gave 650,000 francs to Mr. Perrera's partner, his children received 1,500,000 francs and his parents 150,000 francs. Let us take as an example his parents. These could only in any case plead moral injury; this was much higher than is usually awarded in an internal case for moral injury. This rather high sum should be considered as the price for calming the conscience of the government, or rather the state. If the price of a life is here higher than in other cases, this is because in a way the state was requested to make an act of contrition. There is no interstate penal law. This breach of the law, which France accepted, was righted in one single operation: compensation for injury and for breaking the law. There is a punitive element in the fine that France made itself pay as reparation.

There was a similar rationale from the Americans following the mistake made by the captain of the battleship *Le Vincennes* which mistaking an Iranian Airlines Boeing for a hostile aircraft, fired at the plane which resulted in it exploding and bodies falling into the Persian Gulf from which they were recuperated. The American government proposed a settlement for each passenger. However the Iranian government—in contrast to the Dutch government and Mr. Perrera—did not want a private settlement; they wanted an international case so as to highlight the American responsibility.

Identical situations result in completely different results. Passengers of the Korean Airlines plane shot down by the Soviet air force about 10 years ago, did not benefit from the contrition of the state since the Soviet Union felt that in no way were they responsible. So they could only rely on the goodwill of the company which in fact did compensate the victims but for commercial reasons, since it did not want any problems on its flights and could count on the bulk of payments coming under the Warsaw convention. Once again showing the relativity of the price of a life. The forfeit price of compensation paid for loss of life under the Warsaw Convention in a plane accident is not the same depending on whether the aircraft serves American destinations on a regular basis, since the Americans could not tolerate the idea of a modest ceiling of forfeit for the Warsaw Convention which at the time of the KAL accident was at 8,300 American dollars per person killed. It rose to 75,000 dollars if it involved an airline that regularly serviced America and which would most probably have American citizens aboard.

The responsibility of the state might also be invoked in legal actions. This responsibility in legal actions results in compensation but which also vary greatly. Among the different possible cases let us look at the systems that exist in case of catastrophes such as nuclear explosions. In terms of nuclear explosions, which are extremely rare yet when they occur can set in motion frightening suffering, in which case mechanisms of responsibility could operate although there is no absolute guarantee. This might be rather shocking, however there is no *a priori* responsibility in international law for damages which flow from one country's perfectly legal activity which overflows into another country's territory. This is a clear ethical problem. If there is no convention them there can be no compensation. No country asked for compensation from the Soviet Union for damages suffered following Chernobyl, simply because all countries concerned know that up to now there is no provision in terms of compensation for damage due to nuclear accidents. If an explosion of this sort does happen there will only be compensation for the victims if they are members of countries that have agreed such compensation. There are many great differences! Compensation also has a strict ceiling. In fact there are huge amounts of money set aside for this, compulsory for the operators through insurance companies and furthermore by governments who have given further money to operate it, yet there is even so a ceiling. The sums that are to be used are not the same for the victims depending on where they are in relation to the explosion. Taking Germany as an example, what did they decide? No ceiling for an explosion in Germany affecting people in Germany; a ceiling for explosions that occur in Germany and which affect people who are outside Germany but inside a country that has a convention with Germany; a lower ceiling for victims who are outside Germany but who are not in a country that has a convention with Germany. Depending on where you are, the ceiling being different, if there are a large number of victims the compensation will vary. The amounts are colossal. It is worth noting that they are 5 times as large for the Germans than for the French and 4 times as large for the Americans.

Here are the outlines of the ideas that I wanted to present and which it seems to me show that there is a discrepancy within each judicial system which tends to increase considerably when what lawyers term an extraneous element is introduced into litigation.

North-South: The Money of the Rich and the Money of the Poor

Bernard Maris

A banknote is an acknowledgement of a debt. When speaking of money we in fact are speaking of debts. The debt of the rich (the United States—about 660 billion dollars) is comparable to that of the poor countries of Latin America (420 billion dollars). Yet they are not of the same order: the former corresponds to the credit a rich country gives to itself; the latter is the credit granted by rich countries to the poor.

When Milton Friedman, the 1976 Nobel prize for economics, was asked the question: "Should we be worried that the United States are living on credit?" he replied: "Why should we worry. The deficit is in dollars and not in francs or pounds. In the worst case scenario we can always print more notes." A cynical but superb answer, an overlord's view of the banknote: money is the prince's debt and the prince is only accountable to God. The divine guarantee of money, "We believe in God" is printed on the green note. Nature makes metals, the king creates currency. In the meantime the United States owes nothing.

The poor however have to pay their debts. Why? To get richer no doubt. What concerns us here is the indebtedness as analyzed in the reports of the International Monetary Fund and the World Bank. What do the IMF and WB reports say openly or discretely? A rather hackneyed story, paternalist and reactionary dealing with international relations. In addition the two institutions show the same simple and moralizing attitude to the citizens of the south.

Why Do The Poor Pay?

The Emergence of Debt

The crisis of the debt of southern countries came to light in August 1982 when Mexico declared a suspension of repayment which was soon followed by Brazil. The Mexican fall due was immediately settled by the IMF and the United States.

It would appear that the South owes 600 billion dollars which in all probability will never be repaid. Yet this 600 billion represents approximately the financial surplus that arose out of the petrol crisis of 1973 and 1979. It seems that the "nuisance of the petrol crisis" was passed on by the rich to the poor.

In 1991, the debt of the South was more than 1,400 billion dollars. Yet the South paid up. From 1982 to 1989, the net transfer of capital from Latin America alone reached 150 billion dollars or more depending on the source. In interest alone Brazil paid 100 billion dollars over the period or almost half its exports or in other words 5% of its GDP.

Germany between the wars never had to make such an effort: in 1929 it set aside 2.3% of its GDP in reparations, and 12.6% of its exports; in 1985 Latin America on average put 4.1% of its GDP and 34% of its exports in debt repayment.

THE NORTHERN CARTEL

The IMF managed the Mexican crisis in a remarkable way. The IMF is a body created just after the Second World War, a sort of supervisory body for banks, whose task is to help stabilize the currencies; we also know that, due to the proportions of the shares and votes, the IMF is controlled by the United States and the richest countries. The G7, an informal meeting of Finance ministers (US, France, Great Britain, Germany, Japan, Italy and Canada) alone represents 50% of the votes.

What the IMF managed to achieve in 1982 was a declaration of solidarity on the part of the Northern countries and the creation of a credit cartel. Not only did the rich countries confront the crisis as a group but the European banks, the small banks and the American regional bank which are less implicated than the large American banks, were ordered to take on a collective responsibility of lenders and carry out a rescheduling of the debt. This rescheduling took place in Paris under the auspices of the Treasury. The "Paris Club" resurrected for the occasion, including all the creditor banks, consider problems of debt "individually case by case." Since 1983, the "Paris Club" has rescheduled 180 billion dollars, in other words nothing.

The nightmare for the IMF—and the Paris Club—would be the end of the "case by case" handling. At all costs they need to avoid dealing collectively with debt and even worse would be the formation of a cartel of debtors. For in reality, just as the treating of each case on its individual merit protects the financial community, so a collective moratorium would endanger it. Yet in fact there has never been, not even with the driving force of the "bad poor countries" or rather bad payers (Brazil, Argentina, Peru and Guatemala) even the beginnings of a debtors club.

The Paris Club examines sympathetically requests for rescheduling, in other words the relationship between the interest and the loan, so in fact the devaluing of debts, in return for agreement of policy changes put forward by the IMF. Furthermore at the same time the IMF grants credits to pay off the interest. The north pays—in a minimal way—the north. Its a system of self-insurance.

THE POLICY OF READJUSTING

There are two axis: restrict public expenditure and devalue the national currency. The consequences are disastrous for the most indebted countries. The purchasing power collapses: less than 25% of GDP per capita for Venezuela, Peru and Argentina and 45% for Nicaragua. In fact it is the work force that assures the readjustment. In Mexico the minimum wage went from 120 dollars to 50 and even less in Peru. Since public expenditure is particularly under scrutiny a collapse of the public sector can be seen, investment being the easiest area to rein in rather than current expenditure and the civilian sector easier to contain than the military.

GOOD OR BAD POOR COUNTRIES

From 1982, the doctrine of readjustment was accepted and encouraged by Paul Volcker, the President of the American Federal Bank, the supervisory body of the American credit system. Paul Volcker emphasized that the good payers should benefit from short-term bridging loans and the bad sanctioned. The sanctions are: confiscation of assets, an embargo on foreign trade and above all denying access to the international capital markets.

In fact these sanctions are unworkable. The debt is generally public and not underwritten. An embargo on foreign trade punishes far more the North and also access to capital markets is not hermetic. Therefore it is perfectly feasible to refuse, at least temporarily, responsibility for debt. Peru's decision in 1986 to only repay a 10% of its exports resulted in clear financial benefit. In 1984 Argentina threatened to stop repayments. There followed a crazy rescue operation with Mexico and underwritten by the American treasury. Mexico itself was lending.

As always Mexico is a good pupil. They scrupulously follow the orders of the IMF and await "life after the debt," a phrase coined by one of the finance ministers. Finally in 1987 the World Bank forewent on its debt with Mexico. In 1989, following the "Brady Plan" (see below) Mexico was to receive a further sizable reduction. Yet Brazil which is seen as a bad payer was also to experience a similar sizable reduction in its debt!

Chile and Colombia are also good pupils. Yet the real "favourites" of the North are Poland and Egypt, whose debt would be virtually wiped out, the former as a laboratory for privatization in the east and the latter due to its participation in the coalition that would crush Iraq. Always case by case.

In practice the quality of good or bad pupil does not seem to have any true relevance. This is the problem of stowaways: the bad debtor profits in the same way as the good from a sanitization of debt.

ANNULLING THE DEBT?

From 1985 it was clear that the South would be unable to pay. But, after 1985, the risk of bankruptcy in the North receded. The banks made sufficient provision for bad debt and organized a grey market for debt in which they are renegotiated at a value of 25-50%. Above all the financial markets nowadays value American bank shares as though the South will never have repay.

James Baker in 1985 proposed a relaunch of credits to the South. Then in 1989 Nicholas Brady's plan, bearing his successors name, put forward the proposal to annul two thirds of the debt and guarantee the rest. This proposal was taken up by France and more recently Britain. But what are the reasons for annulling this debt?

Are there economic reasons? No. The banks are saved the bother. The South no longer seems to be so attractive in contrast to Eastern Europe. Of course an improvement in the trade balance might mean competition with the North. Even so France for example who is "generous" with its former colonies has a surplus in trade. The only real economic argument is that the countries of the South are "over strangulated"; they repay less than they would if they had a smaller debt. Too much debt kill-off the debt.

Are there political reasons? No. The question of Nicaragua is settled. It is unlikely that a Marxist regime will establish itself in South America. The region is becoming democratic and democracies are reasonable. Peru, the largest producer of raw cocaine in the world is finally making amends.

Are there ecological reasons? No. Brazil under Sarney together with the World Bank (which suddenly has discovered an ecological side after having favoured the most devastating projects) contemplated renegotiating the debt in exchanged for saving the forests. Yet the Paris Club favours development projects in the hope of being repaid.

There remains only the moral question. This is the Brady Plan for a moratorium on the debt. Unfortunately the morality of the moratorium is not that of the IMF nor of the World Bank.

THE MORALITY OF THE IMF AND WORLD BANK

Reading the reports of the IMF and the World Bank which unfortunately not penned by great writers, there reappears an ancient morality and a reactionary rhetoric. What are the main themes?

FORGIVENESS

"Forgiveness" and forgetting of the debt. This is one of the themes that come out of J. Baker's speech in Seoul in 1985. Forgiveness is what Violeta Chamorro of Nicaragua on a visit to Paris in September asked for (where in Nicaragua the average yearly income is 2,500 francs and where each Nicaraguan owes 15,000 francs). The IMF evokes the "generosity" of creditors in the matter of rescheduling of debt.

PATIENCE

Every report stresses the perseverance of the debtor countries, even though the IMF concedes that the "process of adjustment seems to be running out of steam." Yet, they continue, slowly certain debtor countries have spontaneously seen new foreign investment come their way. Patience is above all macroeconomic stability, then structural reforms and "if necessary the lightening of debt."

IMMATURITY

The theme of Southern childishness is haunting. In relation to the environment the World Bank emphasizes the "irresponsibility" of the poor, forced to abuse the natural resources, deforestation, etc.

But the immaturity of the South is shown above all in its bad management. This is the clearly reactionary theme of the "perverse effect"; the poor countries wanted to do good but the most needy have suffered from their ignorance: "through an irony of fate it is often the social classes that they wished to benefit who in the end suffer most." The Bank mentions three regimes which it often groups together: Chile under Allende (1970-1973), Peru under Garcia (1985-1988), and Brazil under Sarney (1985-1988).

The theme of the perverse result is naturally taken up in looking at necessary readjustments; the South managed things badly and its policies fall hardest on the poorest with the necessity to readjust. The theme of the "hardship and sacrifice" linked to the necessary adjustment harks back to immaturity and childishness through the intermediary of the "punishment" of the adjusting.

Together with the economic immaturity there is the political immaturity. Considering Japan during the Meiji period the World Bank suggests that although the government of the time was not democratically elected, yet the people felt that it was legitimate and that it was able to carry out some great things. In contrast the governments of Chile under Allende or Peru pre-Fujimori are considered "populist" and naturally their management was demagogic and disastrous. The excessive military spending which now is emphasized by the IMF and the World Bank can also be linked to the theme of immaturity.

THE RETURN OF THE PRODIGAL CHILD

When the "donor" countries gather in Paris to deliver certificates of good behavior or distribute encouragement, as in high school disciplinary board meetings or family gathering they praise the effort made by a country or rejoice at the return of the prodigal child. Thus Bolivia has once more been accepted by the financial family. The present celebrity is Peru which has adopted a drastic reform plan since the election of president Fujimori. In return, just like the prodigal son, they are accorded the fatted calf, in other words a bridging loan of 2 billion dollars. They still owe 22 billion.

The theme of the prodigal son appears in the theme of "excessive expenditure" and countries that live "above their means to the extent that the readjustment is inextricably linked to reduction of demand." The return is dependent on the forgiveness of the father who in the meantime continues his usurious methods by lending in the short-term. Usurious methods since all further credits from the IMF (free or almost free) are budget loans to stave off current expenditure for a more and more feeble basket-case. The South exhausts itself in debt to import food so as to pay its backlog: this is usury.

Of the eleven moral virtues put forward by Benjamin Franklin nine are clearly shared by the poor: silence, order, frugalness, moderation, freedom of speech, loyalty, the search for what is useful, moral balance and humility; two alone are not achieved: chastity and cleanliness. About the latter very Nordic idea, Peru paid for its insalubriousness and lack of hygiene with a cholera epidemic which claimed more than two thousand victims. Malaria and white leprosy are spreading swiftly. The North though has reached the pinnacle of a clean war.

FINANCE AND CONFIDENCE: THE REALITY OF PUBLIC FAITH

Robert Lion

A widely held maxim states that money rules in industrialised societies, that cash is ever present and many also add that it spreads corruption. It is easy to believe that money dominates everything and that the world is divided into the haves and the have nots. In France, as in many other countries, if we admit that financial operations are necessary, we must also distinguish between the nature and intended purpose of transactions. As François Mitterand once said, you must distinguish between money that you need and easy money. The former President of France used this phrase on the occasion of the 175th anniversary of the Caisse des dépôts (public savings bank) in September 1991.

However, it is not just a question of putting money to good use, since beyond its undeniable concrete and material utility in measuring and fixing value, money has over the years gained more power, because it requires its users' confidence.

At the same time as this power has grown, the confidence inspired by currency has undergone a change together with that inspired by the world of politics in which it plays a considerable part.

John K. Galbraith recently stated in the *Revue d'économie financière*, "When the possession of money becomes an end in itself, an individual's sole purpose in life, then there is no respect for the law. This is the eternal history of speculation." The great theoretician economics was referring to the 1980s in the United States, when financial scandals severed the link between the real economy and the financial economy as a result of speculation and the Texas oil boom bust in the 1970s, the real estate boom in the 1980s, the era of mega-takeovers and of LBOs (leveraged buy-outs) and the emergence of the junk bonds market.

The crises, scandals and upheavals grew apace in a world dominated by money and financial imperatives. Some economists say the United States has been through its worst financial crisis, worse still than the Wall Street Crash. Savings banks are going out of business and taxpayers will bear the brunt of these bankruptcies for years to come, all because of the ill-timed deregulation of the 1980s.

Millions have been robbed of their life's savings by the bankruptcy of savings banks; hundreds of banks threaten to file for bankruptcy, and one of the states has had to take over some banks, in the wake of a "nationalisation-catastrophe" scenario, to bail out its depositors. There is an all-pervading and ruinous debt crisis, stemming from the federal government, unable to contain the budget deficit. The government's ability to raise money is compromised and the Treasury has had difficulty selling bonds.

There have been thousands of examples of bankruptcy during this century. General and more localized crises proliferate, sometimes spectacularly: hyperinflation to panic selling, excessive volume of debt leading to reneging, stock market crashes; from time to time the big financial institutions teeter, as safety mechanisms fail to function; aided by new technologies improving communication on the global market, speculators go for short term gain at the expense of the future. As happened in years gone by, money and politics corrupt each other, leading to the gain of a few individuals at the expense of the public.

The financial markets are fragile, undermined by speculative fever which has carved up industrial groupings and then turned on the industrialists or the capital holders, who are caught up in these intrigues. Examples come from all over the world, enriched by the dubious mix of politics and money. Even Japan, so upright in appearance, is not immune, even though it has been able to separate the financial sector, ravaged by scandals, from the economy, which remains buoyant.

All these technical phenomena supplement corruption syndromes and lead one to believe that we are about to see a world market completely beyond the law. There are many signs of anxiety. The money laundering activities of the drugs cartels is almost on a par with the world oil market. In Eastern Europe corruption acts as a social system. Developing countries offer further examples of public morality under attack.

The economic and financial worlds need confidence. A stock market cannot function without the confidence of those involved. Especially since today, with super-fast computers and instantaneous global communications, people who have never met but belong to the same profession do lucrative deals knowing they can rely on their opposite numbers to play by the rules. An economic system needs confidence in order to work. Credit flows from trust, and without confidence the market's machinery stalls.

Finance and confidence have always gone together, and credit and distrust run in alternating cycles. How can we think about money, finance and confidence in the middle of all these scandals and tensions?

The Caisse des dépôts (the major savings deposit bank) is deeply concerned with maintaining confidence and public faith. France has known a number of financial crises leading to loss of confidence and the Caisse des dépôts's continued existence, since it was founded in 1816, proves that there are remedies to these crises.

The régime in France at the time of the Second Restoration in 1815 faced enormous difficulties. The new government lacked credibility, the economy was totally destabilised, though not without vigour, and there was no credit available. It was a matter of urgency to build up confidence in every sphere, but mainly in the financial sector. The bankruptcy of the public finances had brought about the absolute monarchy's downfall and provided the fuse for the Revolution. Successive revolutionary governments had tried to address the problem before the whole edifice foundered under the Directorate with "the bankruptcy of two-thirds." The Consulate and Empire had begun to build a more efficient financial system with the Banque de France and the Caisse d'amortissements (sinking fund) being established in 1800, but the Hundred Days of Napoleon had revived many fears. Before the final defeat, Napoleon had emptied the most forbidden coffers, using up the sinking fund and the Deposit and Consignment Office funds.

The nation-state had enormous needs in 1815: it was occupied by coalition forces holding it to ransom; creditors were still awaiting settlement of Ancien Regime debts; and the Treasury was empty. In this uncertain and volatile political climate, it was impossible to raise taxes so the state had to borrow money and no one was willing to extend any credit.

The government made a bold move and bet on confidence. It passed a Finance Act in 1816, which was the first public finance code in France's history, and established two institutions which proved the bedrock of their campaign to raise confidence: the Caisse d'amortissements (sinking fund) and the Caisse des dépôts et consignations (Deposit and Consignment Office).

The Caisse d'amortissements was the best guarantee for the successful borrowing of the necessary funds; the Caisse des dépôts et consignations was active proof of the state's credibility and resuscitated public credit. This institution was a safe place for all citizens to deposit the money put aside voluntarily and as a bond, as well as savings for the future.

Thus the double effect of the security of the depositors en masse, who have no access to banks which did not exist as such in those days, and the collective utility of their funds, meant that state credit was secured and the economy boosted: progress was in sight.

The Caisse des dépôts had particular mechanisms to inspire and maintain confidence. The same director general was there to defend the inviolability of both institutions. Both history and the current situation demanded that the director general's ability to say "No" guaranteed the caisses' security and integrity. He could prevent the government's demands on the pennies he watched over. This incredible power guarantees success and corresponds, in a more modest way, to the charter, the 1814 Constitution, which gave the King his right of veto. The predecessors of the caisses' director general, in the 18th century and under the Empire, were unable to stand up to the arbitrary demands of the executive powers, which severely weakened credit but also savings, public credit and revenue.

This independent status originated in experience, the urgency at the time, and wisdom with regard to a longer view and was as unusual then as it is today. There was one purpose: giving the director general the maximum independence as the guardian of the "citizens' sacred treasure" and guarantor of the nation's confidence. The director general was appointed by the King as head of state but he was not accountable to the executive, the Ministry of Finance. His appointment was not for a fixed term, so he did not have to curry favour with anyone to assure another term. He was, however, not without check. The law gave him as a supervisor the legislature, parliament, representing the nation and the citizens.

Article 115 of the 1816 law stated "the Caisse des dépôts et consignations is placed, in a most special way, under the guidance of the legislative authority as well as benefiting from its guarantee." This arrangement, innovative for its time, drew its inspiration from ancient democracy as well as Montesquieu's theories and other political philosophers' ideas. Who better to supervise the management of the citizens' money, the nation's fortune, than the nation's representatives and legislators who "express the people's will."

The legislators went further in putting the Caisse des dépôts in the nation's hands. Not only does parliament exercise its supervisory jurisdiction but a commission including members of parliament, state representatives and representatives of economic institutions also supervises its actions as well as public opinion. The *Journal officiel* (Official Journal) published its results every quarter, a considerable innovation at the time.

From the start, what we now call transparency was the guiding principle behind the management of the Caisse des dépôts. There was almost an obligation to be public.

In early society public faith, with its definite rites, was the religion of confidence. This was as true in olden times as it was in 1816 and it remains thus to this day. The director general's oath sums up the solemnity with which he pledges the nation. The oath is the sacred guarantee of the Caisse des dépôts et consignations and echoes ancient cults of public faith. The explanatory text of the 1816 law stated "There is no safer place for depositing shares than in a fund guaranteed by public faith."

The notion of public faith has a long history. It goes back to the earliest civilizations, to the primitive foundations of debt and contract. Rome deified it in its pantheon, at the first king and lawgiver Numa's instigation. According to Plutarch, he "made the Romans understand that the holiest and most important oath they could make was to pledge their faith." Public faith had its temple on the Capitol, and diplomatic treaties were deposited there as well as deposits and goods which citizens consecrated to the goddess. *Fides publica*, the Roman people's faith, demonstrated confidence in both its meanings—the confidence emanating from the people and that demanded of others and the state. Public faith is also the sanctifying of the social bond, the taboo symbol of collective endeavour, the mark of a unified nation.

In more recent times public faith is invoked when the state requires credit. Genoa and Venice, in the 16th century, both founded national banks *sotto la fede publica*.

When enlightened Europe paved the way for revolutions, this age-old adage became rejuvenated. In the 18th century confidence became an essential tool of government and the English were the first to demonstrate this with the founding of the Bank of England, their secret weapon for some time. Absolutist France was unable to adapt to this financial revolution and this impotence eventually led to a more radical revolution at the end of the century. However among philosophers, pamphleteers, mathematicians, and financiers the prevailing conviction was that the people's confidence was the only possible guarantee of healthy public finances. The only existing form of public credit is that extended by the people, resting on the nation's faith. Public opinion desired liberty and equality and this led to anxiety about financial equity, a pledge of security for governments. Savings and, that which insures the other revolutionary notion, providence, both demand public faith in order to redeem the national debt and improve the lot of poor people.

But this does not fit the facts in France. On the contrary, before 1789, the state's credit was in tatters and Paris as a financial center was corrupted by speculation. In these circumstances, public faith became the mobilising cry of the Revolution. At the opening of the Estates General, Necker declared "public confidence is unsettled, yet this confidence is vitally necessary: it honors the nation and represents its political vigour." Two months later, on the eve of the capture of the Bastille prison, the National Assembly announced that "no one has the right to utter the infamous word of 'bankruptcy,' no one has the right to undermine the public faith in whatever form it takes and whatever its denomination."

The assemblies did not resound to the sacred words of public faith again until 1815. When Minister Corvetto proposed the creation of the Caisse des dépôts et consignations and the Caisse d'amortissements, he recalled the old principle "Debt is sacred, it rests on public faith. That is the price to be paid to restore the government's credit. Public confidence will re-establish an equilibrium, based on the inviolability of the faith secured by our sacred promises."

The Caisse des dépôts represented the concretization of public faith, which became operational. This restoration of finances and credit remains an astonishing feat in French history and the 1816 arrangement has preserved to this day its almost miraculous nature. In a few years, the debt redeeming mechanism freed the country from its debts and reinvigorated borrowing in an unprecedented way. In a few years the "dépositaire general," the Caisse des consignations, as it was known at the time, operated successfully on the market and impressed public opinion.

According to the models drawn up by 18th century experts and financiers, the Caisse acted to concentrate and coordinate the new spirit of providence, offered a safe place for citizens' meagerly savings to prosper. Despite not taking up the challenge in 1816, but after constant pressure from interested parties, the Caisse des dépôts began to manage savings banks' funds in 1837. Lamartine had long pressed that "the workers' precious deposits should be entrusted to the inviolable guardian of the nation's treasure."

Shortly after, France decided to enlarge the scope of providence because of mounting social pressures: the need to offer the working classes a pension for their old age. Again the Caisse des dépôts et consignations had its part to play. The revolution of 1848 led to a Caisse for old age pensions as well as friendly societies, which decided to place their funds with the Caisse des dépôts. The Second Empire followed up this financial and social endeavour and brought together all the providential institutions' funds that the state had set up within the Caisse des dépôts. This capital belonged to the people and needed 30 years of security to generate a profitable return. This concentration stabilized the public finances and helped debt management.

Despite changes in regimes and generations, the Caisse des dépôts vindicated itself as the guardian of public faith. In 1848, Goudchaux, the Finance Minister, paid tribute to "this institution which holds the public confidence." Over the years "clients" have come and gone, from lawyers in 1890 and official liquidators in 1985, or more recently in the summer of 1991 hospital funds, which had been depositing money since 1816. This occurred because nowhere else can offer such security and because for the lawmakers of the present day, nowhere else does finance rhyme so well with confidence.

It has to be said that savers whose funds are held by the Caisse des dépôts have never experienced any difficulties. Those with a cashbook type A, representing 700 billions on deposit, can always make immediate withdrawals without prior notice of deposits and can expect regular payments of interest due (no small sum at almost 30 billion francs a year).

It is the institution's independence that is largely responsible for this state of affairs. In these days of budgetary largesse, both the law and the oath support each other so the Caisse des dépôts remains the bastion built by its founders. In 1816 they said "Confidence cannot be imposed from above." This institution is no stranger to the fact that there is confidence in the French financial system.

If any two words can sum up the achievements of the Caisse des dépôts et consignations, founded on the principles of utility and security, they are revenue and roads. The Caisse's founders intended it to contribute to the state's financial stability by maintaining revenues, thanks to its links with the Caisse d'amortissements, as well as to the general well-being by financing the building of the infrastructure, from royal roads to canals in 1816 to the public works of the July monarchy.

Regarding revenue and roads, it is the same today when the French Treasury is offered powerful support in the management of its debt and through the subsidiaries CLF and C3D the institution presses for local development.

In 1837, hundreds of savings banks funds joined the Caisse des dépôts. The lawmakers intended it to act as a haven of safety as well as an efficient way to promote to common good. The Caisse provided over a long period of time cash advances to the Treasury to finance major developments: in the 1870s the highways, local roads, in the 1880s schools, then at the start of the 20th century the supply of water and also electricity to rural areas. Very prudently it was only in 1931 that the lawmakers and the Caisse allowed the savings banks' funds to be used to make loans to local government and towns. Since 1950, these funds have contributed to the rebuilding and modernization of the country during three "glorious" decades of expansion.

Nowadays, the money flowing into the savings banks is scarcer (I mean the main resource, the untaxed cash books), yet the state is asking for funding for the general welfare by building housing projects. This resource is untaxed: the state decides what it should be used for; only for the masses; it leaves the detail to the Caisse; it requires that the Caisse keeps things in balance and acts as a security device which brings us back to public faith. This is no small matter: this transformation—on the one side the cash books, on the other 30-year loans—is unique. Some 550 billion francs make up long-term loans. The state's guarantee on the cash books is the ultimate source of confidence: but for the Caisse des dépôts if there were recourse to the state—it has never happened—this would by the ultimate dishonour.

Even though the secular dispositions and the destination of savings banks' funds are agreed in conjunction with the state authorities, the Caisse des dépôts, in line with the wishes and instructions of its 1816 founders, operates completely independently when it comes to its "general section" funds, those which tally with the services decided on at the start. This freedom, which has never been curbed, is the precondition of the institution's independence as well as the security of the capital entrusted to it, engaging its responsibility. particularly that of its director general. The Caisse also plays fully its main role as inviolable depository of the nation. It has always looked for uses which have the double advantage of security and returns, state securities, of course, but also canals, ports, roads and rivers, during its early years and nowadays investments in skyscrapers or forests, in real estate, held as debentures, also made up of stocks from the sectors in the throes of development.

Little by little, following economic and social changes in France, the Caisse des dépôts has intervened in many sectors. But many of the areas wherein it practices its modern craft come from the more distant past.

With the Caisse nationale de prevoyance (CNP), the Caisse provides life insurance, having taken over the task entrusted to the first institutions born of the 1848 Revolution, which the Republican state decided was its responsibility, namely to look after the insurance needs of the poorest peoples. For almost a century, until the advent of social security in 1945, the Caisse des dépôts was the almost exclusive instrument of public providence, and during the 1937 world exhibition, it was claimed to be world's largest providential and insurance institution. Today the CNP is realigning itself in its sphere, but it will always retain that spirit of generosity to its citizens, inspired in 1848 at its birth.

In the same way, we have inherited since the start of retirement provisions substantial funds. It can be said that one in seven Frenchmen and women depends on the Caisse des dépôts for his/her retirement.

It is also the headquarters of many service industries. This is the result of François Bloch-Laine's initiative in the 1950s, when post-war France needed housing, highways, and major redevelopments. No one, neither the state nor the market, was in a position to meet these urgent needs, and the Caisse played a pioneering role, by intervening through its "technical subsidiaries." Today these industries survive the disciplines of the market—and some fall by the wayside—without enjoying a monopoly or other privileges, but they offer this bonus: the values of the group of the Caisse des dépôts and the 1816 traditions.

The Caisse des dépôts is also a shareholder in many companies. Since 1816 it did so within strict confines but since 1931, it has been legally allowed to buy shares, even for the savings banks funds. Its first significant purchase was in the Compagnie des wagons-lits (sleeping cars), which allowed France to participate in Europe's new industrial organizations and to balance international groupings.

When they are handled carefully, these investments are profitable, resulting in gains for the funds we manage. Lighter than investments in bond-holding or interest rate products—the Caisse holds 13 percent of French bond holdings, but only 3 percent of share capital—they constitute a part of our assets, the institutional investor's face who has often been asked to become the Stock Exchange's policeman, when it is really the leader of the regulatory syndicate on difficult days. Apart from a few exceptions, these policies are nothing more than investments, which we manage in order to get the highest profit—over a space of time of variable length—for the funds that back them up.

Today we manage these funds with open eyes by not refusing to take part when a take-over bid means that shares we hold are the subject of a stock-market battle; then after taking the advice from the public authorities—who generally fall back on silence—we take into account French economic interests or the combatants' industrial potential.

There are very few sectors of shareholding, in the sense of holding portfolios which we manage directly, being represented on administrative councils and taking part in the life of the enterprise. They are limited to communications and tourism: five or six large enterprises, and a few capital-risk investments. In this particular field, where the risks in financial terms are less than 0.5 percent of the assets managed by the Caisse, some 5 to 6 billion francs out of a total of 1,600 billion, I have suggested the introduction of measures which would control and improve our decision-making.

All this makes up a framework which is impressive but can seem disparate. It is based on an axis with two routes which informs all our actions: security, which fosters confidence, and protects the innumerable savers' cents, as well as utility, which meets our obligation to make this private money grow for the benefit of all.

Over the 175 years the putting into effect of these principles has changed as the world has changed. You have to move with the times. The 1980s were a time of great changes. At the same time we had to retain our core, otherwise we would have become banal, and we would have lost our special status. It was not enough to trumpet the virtues of public faith, we had to make sure this was alive and maintained, in a time of globalization and exceptional crises.

In a world where confidence is under threat, particularly in the financial sector, public faith is in crisis. This explains the drop in savings, a reluctance to invest in the long term, and government credit often precarious. Despite the legislative arsenal aimed at protecting savings, the financial institutions do not inspire confidence. Furthermore given the short-termism, it does not ensure the financing of the economy.

Thus confidence in the financial mechanisms is compromised if not destroyed. The two pillars of the Western economy, the market and the contract, have both been abused and thereby undermined. Hasty deregulation allowed imprudent investments, blameworthy practices or even legal speculation, as can be seen with the malpractices of American lawyers. All this is now being called into question.

But is it perhaps too late? Will the fragility of the financial world survive if the developed world no longer grows economically—as may be the case—in the same way it did since World War II? Savings are in decline and can no longer cover the necessary investments, which endangers the whole economy. There may far-reaching disasters, capable of spreading, which will affect both individuals and the state, because there are not sufficient strong regulators.

To restore legitimacy to public faith, you must first work at the nations' prosperity. According to the brilliant analyses of the 18th century economists, only stable savings, constituting a mass of capital available for investments, can ensure economic development.

This accords with an emerging trend in current Western thinking. There now exists a new demand for state controls and there is a general move toward greater regulation. Morality has found a place in the market and has led to increasingly rigorous standards of professional conduct. Savers have greater access to information. Some institutions pay great store in providing information about investments, indexes, evaluations, and transparency. Another current theme is greater protecting to contracting parties, to investors, and to subscribers. Mechanisms to ensure secure investments have found their limit, particularly in the United States, where the current mishaps of mutual guarantee funds affected the government's budget, demonstrating that security cannot be bought by an insurance scheme. The move to greater protection affects insurance and the financial markets.

Would public faith, supported by public institutions, have prevented the widespread bankruptcies in the United States? According to John K. Galbraith it would have done. He explained that the institutions' first role is the establish a standard of soberness, without any connection with a private institution. "They have to practise," continued Galbraith, "long-termism and think about the collective good. For a nation to have this type of institution means it has a unique advantage in avoiding the bankruptcies, which my country is currently undergoing. These public institutions inspire consumer confidence which is fundamental to the work of finance."

The international situation accentuates this necessity, particularly events in the former Soviet Union and Eastern Europe. After 40 years of Cold War, development is the key word. All the states are competing with one another to do more or less well and build up an important financial structure. In addition, Third World countries will not indefinitely accept inequality nor accept second-class aid. But questions of development bring us back to confidence and the necessary stabilisation of financial systems.

Public faith today also depends on the general state of the economy. When industry is competitive, when the balance of trade is in surplus, when government spending and the public borrowing requirement are under control, when the management of the national debt allows for the greatest credit, when monetary indicators are healthy and interest rates have been set with skill, when the financial markets are healthy and transparent, as well as dynamic and attractive, when the rule of law is sound in relation to financial activities, and, finally, when inflation is kept in check and money is stable and in good repute, then you know that there is confidence.

This means the necessary security to ensure people save their money. No one fears for the deposits or insurance contracts held by competent institutions. The people respond to public faith and to a good policy mix. Today in the era of sophistication, overlaps and internationalisation, this is an altogether more technical and complex operation than 25 centuries ago when the Romans entrusted their money to the *Fides publica*.

There are no economic paradises today. You cannot govern competition, budget surpluses, or exchange rates, etc. You cannot balance a budget without a solid political set-up; you cannot have a sound economy without political stability and political stability does not come easily.

You need to establish a virtuous circle between a courageous and enlightened, firm and consensual political climate and financial security. These form the building blocks which only lack the cornerstone, confidence.

For more general and universal reasons than those which rule the race for the highest return, every citizen should be able to put part or all of his/her savings somewhere without the risk of losing it as happens on the money markets. Every country should look after these deposits, mainly family investments. Our A account is an example of this: centralised with the Caisse des dépôts and it can only be used in investments guaranteed by a local authority or district (yet another example of public faith, as is shown by the legal organization or the system), it offers a modest return, but the community guarantees to reimburse the money immediately and without notice, without its value being diminished by inflation.

In the face of the inherent risks of the financial markets, it is useful that this set-up can guarantee that savings which need to be safe rather than profitable can be made. All nations should ensure this kind of set-up is available. In France all that is needed is that the existing system survives the attempts to abolish it.

Public faith is important. But when periods of relatively healthy finances have hidden its necessity, it is not appreciated until there is a crisis and then it is too late.

